CONTENTS

TABLES

PREFACE

Much of the information in this monograph has been presented at state and national educational computer conferences. The reason for publishing this information is that the response by educators has been enthusiastic. More than one administrator has told me that I have the key to unlock widespread computer use by classroom teachers. A computer software area marketing manager saw this information as a breakthrough to classroom computer use. This book is the result of educator and computer marketing interest.

The objective of this book is to assist educators and teachers to integrate computers into classroom instruction in a reliable, academically sound, and facile manner. The information in this book will assist school and district administrators and others who are responsible for computer-related leadership to successfully enable teachers to integrate computers into their daily classroom activities. Suggestions will be offered that will enable computer software marketers to successfully assist classroom teachers to integrate computers into their daily classroom instruction.

This monograph is particularly directed toward those educators involved in teacher computer preservice and in-service programs and instructional personnel involved with computer support. Those educators involved in computer assistance to teachers may include principals, district administrators, instructional design technologists, researchers, and faculties of education involved in teacher preservice and in-service training. This book will also be of assistance to teachers who are integrating computers into their classroom without support personnel to assist them. The integration of computers into the classroom curriculum is one of the most challenging activities that administrators and teachers face today.

Students are saturated with visual images and spatial activities well before they begin school. Upon entering school the mode of learning abruptly changes to a static experience that actually retards previous connections that have been established in the developing brain. For most students, attending school is a new and often disappointing experience that cannot compete with the visual and spatial activities to which their minds have been previously attuned. Interactive computer/video and visual/spatial images and responses form complex ways of thinking about and reacting to information that the average classroom does not duplicate. Therefore, they must learn new ways of thinking.

With the advent of computers into education, it has become necessary for teachers to learn new patterns of teaching and for software companies to design more interactive and spatially oriented educational products. It has also become necessary for administrators to assist teachers with instructional design and classroom teaching strategies appropriate to the integration of computers into the classroom curriculum.

The purpose of this monograph is to assist district and school-level administrators, faculties at teacher training institutions, and teachers to fully and effectively integrate computers into their classroom curriculum. Each of these groups brings a different perspective of computers to education; however, all of these groups have the same goal of assisting classroom teachers to fully integrate computers into the instructional process.

There are several key concepts that are common to each of these groups. These recommendations will provide the enabling keys to integrate computers into the classroom that are common to each of these groups or to anyone involved with computers in education. This book is based on research and experienced educational practice, and will address specific concerns of classroom teachers at each grade level K-12 concerning the integration of computers into their daily instruction. This monograph will also offer recommendations for administrators to plan and implement programs that will facilitate the use of computers by the classroom teacher.

The philosophy set forth in this monograph is that teachers, rather than administrators, should state what their needs are for computer use. In-service instructional computer programs must be designed, beginning with teachers' perceived computer needs, rather than as is currently done, with administrators designing in-service programs for teachers without understanding which computer skills they desire or need. Until effective programs of teacher in-service and support are designed, it is this author's prediction that computers will not be successfully integrated into the classroom curriculum.

This book was written especially for educators who are interested in the answers to the following questions. The following were some of the questions answered by 728 classroom teachers who participated in a doctoral survey concerning teachers' perceived needs to integrate computers into the classroom.

- In which computer strategies do teachers wish more training?
- In which subject areas do teachers use computers most of the time to support instruction?
- At which levels of education, K-3, 4-6, 7-8, 9-12, do students use computers most of the time?

The importance of these questions lies in the fact that they are asked by a large number of educators. The answers to these questions hold the key to classroom computer use. This book will synthesize the answers to these questions with practical classroom instructional strategies and with recommendations for conducting preservice and in-service training for classroom teachers. Chapters 1-4 present a background of research findings concerning classroom computer use. Chapters 5-9 offer general guidelines to utilize when implementing computers into classroom instruction. Chapters 10-13 offer a master plan for designing computer in-service for classroom teachers. Chapter 14 offers guidelines for national computer in-service standards for teachers.

INTRODUCTION

I served as a library and media director for twenty-three years. This position offered me an opportunity to work closely with teachers, to observe them, and to assist them with their instructional computer needs. This position also offered me opportunities to work with a district technology committee.

Since 1967, I have served in the educational system in California. I have worked with classroom teachers, with administrators, and with college professors. I have served at all levels of education. While working full time as a library and media director, I earned a master's degree in education from California State University, Long Beach; a master's in library science; and a doctorate in education with a major in instructional technology from the University of Southern California.

In 1989, while working full time in the public school system, I began teaching in the California State University System as an adjunct professor in a school of library and information science. In this position, I had further opportunity to work with teachers in the public school system at all grade levels. I have worked as a consultant for the California State Department of Education and conducted seminars and workshops for the Computer Using Educators, California Media and Library Educators Association, and for the International Society for Technology in Education.

During these thirty years in education, I have not seen many changes in the classroom. I have seen administrators and change agents attempting to implement changes; however, the majority of teachers were apathetic or opposed to the attempted changes. The majority of teachers remained ensconced in the traditional methods of instruction.

I have been a member of committees to plan instructional computer use; conducted workshops and seminars at the local, state, and national levels; and worked with numerous teachers and administrators in staff development training programs. I have observed teachers who were enthusiastic about utilizing computers in their classroom, but who soon became disillusioned with the constraints that were imposed upon them. Their enthusiasm was not sustained because of a lack of administrative support and a lack of knowledge of how to integrate computers into instruction.

The majority of teachers who have attempted to integrate computers into their classroom instruction have had to acquire their training on their own time, with their personal funds, and have often had to bring their personal computers from home into their classroom. In other cases, in order to have access to a computer, teachers have had to conduct their instruction in the computer lab. So much time is consumed in moving the class to the lab that there is not enough instructional time left to conduct quality instruction. Also, when using the computer lab, teachers are most often teaching hands-on skills and teaching about the computer; they are not integrating the computer into their classroom curriculum.

As a university professor, I taught library and information science to practicing teachers and library paraprofessionals. These teachers were quite eager to integrate computers into their classes; however, they lacked the basic knowledge of how to do so easily. One of my most popular units was the integration of computers into the classroom.

I have been able to learn first-hand what the major instructional problems are with the integration of computers into the classroom through class discussions and the personal experiences of teachers. They are many. There are problems that are frustrating and problems that stifle enthusiasm; however, these problems can be easily addressed once administrators are fully aware of them.

This book will focus upon the instructional problems of computer integration that were identified by teachers of an average school district as their concerns for the integration of computers into the classroom. By addressing these identified problems, administrators will enable teachers to integrate computers into the classroom on a widespread basis.

This book has grown directly from my experience of the past thirty years. Working with classroom teachers has given me a perspective on the very real problems of computer integration into instruction. Working at the university level has given me the opportunity to view computer use with a broader perspective. As a library and media director, I learned about the time and the energy involved for teachers to integrate computers into their classroom, and from the research for my doctorate, I have gained a research perspective. As a member of a district technology committee, I have gained an understanding of the problems faced by district level personnel responsible for computer integration in their schools.

The problems are the same as the ones I encountered in the early stages of implementing computers in the schools. Instructional computer use in the classroom still remains spotty and often peripheral to the curriculum. School districts still do not know how to approach staff development to train teachers effectively to integrate computers into classrooms on a widespread scale. From working directly with classroom teachers, I have learned what the solutions are to the problems of integrating computers into the classroom.

This book is a summary of thirty years' experience of working in education. I believe this book will offer a breakthrough for all personnel involved in the integration of computers into the classroom.

Chapter 1

COMPUTERS, TEACHERS, AND IN-SERVICE TRAINING

The number of computers in American public schools has increased dramatically over the past decade. In 1982, the number of micro-computers in American schools was estimated to be over 100,000.[1] The preliminary results of United States participation in the 1989 IEA Computers in Education, of 1,400 elementary, middle, and secondary schools conducted by Becker show that schools have added 300,000 to 400,000 computers each year since 1985.[2]

In 1984, Alfred Bork predicted that within twenty years computers would be the major delivery system for education at all levels for most subject areas, and that computers would replace books and the lecture method.[3] The National Commission of Excellence in Education called for schools to treat computing as the fourth "R." This commission also states that computer literacy should be one of the basics required for all high school graduates.

For the 1989-90 school year, Quality Education Data (QED) found that the number of microcomputers in American public schools was 1,822,766.[4] Kinnaman states that virtually all schools in America own computers.[5] Although the numbers of computers in American schools is not evenly distributed, all schools own at least one computer for instructional use. QED found that the ratio of students to computers has rapidly fallen from 125 to 1 during the 1983-84 school year to 22 to 1 in the 1989-90 school year.[6]

In 1988, the Office of Technology Assessment showed that, on the average, there was 1 computer for every 30 students.[7] As of May 1991, there were approximately 2.7 million computers in U.S. public schools.[8] This is approximately 1 computer to every 16 students. QED states that the computer/student ratio will fall to 9 to 1 in the 1995-96 school year.[9]

We can observe that computers are changing the educational experience for teachers, however slowly. In the late 1970s, even a single computer was a novelty in most elementary schools. In secondary schools few computers were in the academic classroom; they were found mostly in computer labs. Educators have become significantly aware of computers in instruction. Currently, there are numerous computers-in-education conferences, and the professional literature contains thousands of articles pertaining to computers-in-education. More than 13,000 educators are members of the International Council for Computers in Education. It is unusual to browse through an educational journal without seeing a computers-in-education conference with sessions on the integration of computers into the classroom. Computers are now standard equipment in U.S. schools with 85 percent of elementary schools and 97 percent of secondary schools owning a computer that is used for instruction.

Computers are in the schools; however, they are not in the classrooms, where most teachers are. They are in areas away from the classrooms, where specialized personnel are utilizing them. The majority of computers have been placed in computer labs, media centers, and administrative offices. Computers are being used to teach keyboarding and computer literacy, to conduct simplified research, and for administrative bookkeeping functions. These are important uses, but they are not classroom centered

There are two specific reasons for the current placement of computers. There are not enough funds to place a computer in every classroom, and teachers still prefer the old teaching methods for routine classroom instruction. The average classroom teacher is not computer literate and cannot utilize computers fully in the basic academic curriculum. As a result, the many computers that have been placed in schools are not being utilized to full capacity.

In 1989, a survey of educational technology use in California K-12 schools was conducted by the California Technology Project (CTP). In this survey, Main and Roberts found that 27 percent of California teachers felt that they lacked computer proficiency. Moreover, over half of the teachers were rated as having limited computer proficiency and one-third were rated unskilled for both personal computer and instructional computer use. A major problem area cited in the results of the CTP study was the integration of computers into the curriculum.[10] Ninety-one percent of California teachers felt that the integration of computers into their classroom curriculum was a serious problem for them, because they believed that they were lacking in computer proficiencies. Bruwelheide found that there was no consensus regarding the competencies needed by classroom teachers for successful computer use in the classroom. Furthermore, Bruwelheide found that most researchers differ on the kind of instruction needed by teachers to achieve computer literacy.[11]

In 1988, it was estimated that in about 75 percent of schools with computers, teachers were actually using the computers for instructional purposes less than one half of the time.[12] Some researchers found that many teachers have become overwhelmed by the rapid placement of computers into schools.[13] Teachers are also reluctant to use computers because of educational problems concerning their use in whole class instruction. O'Donnell found that teachers perceived themselves to be at a beginning level of computer use and that they were concerned about the use of computers in their daily instruction with student groups. O'Donnell also found that computer use among respondents was low and that computers were not being used to their fullest potential.[14]

Past and current research has addressed the problem of teacher computer proficiency from a top-down perspective without fully considering teachers' perceptions of their need to integrate computers into the instructional process. A study conducted by the University of Oregon Mainstreaming Computers Project from 1968-1980 found that teacher participation is necessary for successful implementation of all phases of computer programs. Becker found that any intervention process must include all of the teachers.[15]

Specific identification of the proficiencies and strategies that teachers believe are needed to integrate computers into the classroom would give required direction to in-service training and allow a more scientific approach to the problem of integrating computers into the classroom curriculum. Although many school districts have made a valiant effort toward integration of computers into classroom instruction with in-service programs and master technology plans, computers still are not being used by classroom teachers on a regular basis in their daily instruction. Also, the majority of teachers who are utilizing computers in their instruction have not fully integrated them into the curriculum but have only incorporated the computer with little change in actual curriculum and classroom strategies.

Lack of Computer Use by Teachers

With the dramatic increase in the number of computers in American schools, it would be reasonable to assume that microcomputer use by teachers has also increased. However, as shown above, this is not the case. Educators and experts in the field agree that the impact of computer use upon education is minimal. Effective and innovative computer use in classrooms can be found, but it is rare.[16] Luning states that merely having computers in schools does not increase their use.[17] In 1988, the Office of Technology Assessment reported that only one-half of the nation's teachers have ever used a computer.[18] However, in 1989, twice as many teachers than in 1988 indicated that they were using computers for instruction. Only 64 percent of teachers who had access to computers actually used them.[19] Becker has noted that instructional computer use remains episodic and peripheral to the regular program of instruction.[20]

Winkler found that computers may be available in U.S. public schools, but he questions whether they are being used wisely or well. Winkler also believes that the computer is not being used as a tool for improving instruction in subject matter courses and that when computers are utilized as an instructional tool, their use is often restricted to skill mastery, drill and practice, and tutorials that are not fully integrated into the instructional process.[21] In addition, Winkler believes that the teacher should be provided with centralized, routine assistance in integrating computers into the curriculum.[22]

In 1989, Main and Roberts found that out of 432 teachers surveyed, 91 percent felt that the integration of computers into their classroom instruction was a serious problem for them.[23] Over half of California teachers are rated by Main and Roberts as being of limited proficiency or unskilled in both personal computer productivity and instructional computer use.[24] Moursund believes that computers have had a very modest impact upon instruction, with the typical high school graduate having had little or no interaction with computers in a classroom.[25]

Robbat states that two years after the inauguration of a computer program to utilize computers for instructional use, teachers lost their enthusiasm. Eight computers and eight printers, purchased with grant funds, were placed in the classrooms of eight social science teachers. The teachers received in-service training to familiarize them with various ways to use the computer and the printer.[26] One of the goals was to encourage these teachers to utilize the computer as an instructional tool for students in their classrooms. Robbat also states that only one teacher had success utilizing the computer in the classroom curriculum and that the results of instructional computer use are disappointing.[27] For most of the teachers in the social science department, having access to a computer in the classroom had no meaningful impact on education. Robbat also notes that the equipment and the software sit unused most of the time. Teachers received in-service training; however, it would seem that it did not meet their needs. Robbat believes that this is a common occurrence in schools.[28]

In a statewide survey of school districts in Michigan, Stemmer and Carlson noted that 50 percent of teachers reported that they never use computers in their classrooms, 30 percent occasionally use computers, and only 20 percent frequently use computers in their instruction.[29] Although computers are in American public schools, their use by teachers for instruction is not widespread.

Major Problems with the Integration of Computers

Major problems are associated with the integration of computers into the classroom. Moursund states that educators mistakenly believe that just introducing microcomputers into the classroom is sufficient.[30] However, even after large numbers of computers have been placed in America's classrooms, the extent of microcomputer use in classroom instruction is still disappointing.

A study of the problems of integrating computers into the classroom has yielded a multiplicity of factors, with one outstanding problem being identified. Fawson and Van Uitert state that the lack of teacher training is a major reason why teachers are not utilizing microcomputers to a greater extent in classroom instruction.[31] Bruder, the Director of the Kentucky Department of Education's unit for Mathematics and Technology, states that although interest in technology is at an all-time high, unless strong emphasis is placed on teacher training to implement successful programs, computer use in classrooms will not occur.[32]

The Association for Computing Machinery Committee, Elementary and Secondary Subcommittee was created to identify major problems of integrating computers into classroom instruction.[33] Under the direction of Moursund, a survey was conducted of persons in education who were asked to discuss what they saw as some major problems of the instructional use of computers in the classroom. The results of this survey showed that the lack of adequately trained teachers was seen as the most widespread problem in the integration of computers into the classroom. Moursund also found that without knowledgeable and supportive teachers, the placement of computers in schools will be disappointing and will result in failure.[34]

In a survey of school districts in California for the Rand Corporation, Stasz found that over 60 percent of teachers using computers were either unprepared or inadequately prepared.[35] Over three quarters of the districts not using computers reported that the faculty had very little preparation in instructional computer use. Stutzman reported that the most reported obstacle to instructional computer use was a lack of funds, followed by a lack of adequately trained teachers.[36] In-service training is being conducted by the majority of school districts. However, even with in-service training, computer use by classroom teachers is negligible. In-service alone is not the answer. It is the manner in which it is designed, developed, and conducted that is the key factor to successful in-service. In-service for computer integration requires a new direction, with programs that focus specifically upon the whole class instructional needs of the teachers, and with an emphasis upon the actual identified needs of the classroom teachers who are to participate in the training.

NOTES

1. J. Lipkin, "A Teacher and a Place," *Education Times* 1, no.7 (1982): 7-9.
2. H. J. Becker, *IEA Computers in Education Survey* (Baltimore, MD: The John Hopkins University, Center for Social Organization of Schools, 1990).
3. A. Bork, "Computer Futures for Education." *Creative Computing* 10, no. 11 (1984): 178-180.
4. Quality Education Data, *Microcomputer Usage in Schools, a QED 1989-90 Update* (Denver, CO: A Peterson Company, 1991): 30
5. D. Kinnaman, "What's the Research Telling Us?" *Classroom Computer Learning* 10, no. 6 (1990): 31- 35.
6. Quality Education Data, *Microcomputer Usage*, 30.
7. Office of Technology Assessment, *Power On! New Tools For Teaching and Learning* (Publication No. 052-003-01125-5) (Washington, DC: U.S. Government Printing Office, 1988).
8. P. Elmer-Dewitt, "The revolution that fizzled," *Time* (20 May 1991): 48-49.
9. Quality Education Data, *Microcomputer Usage, 30.*

10. R. Main and L. Roberts, "An Assessment of Educational Applications in California Public Schools: Benchmark Survey," *California Technology Project* 1, no. 2 (July 1990): 17
11. J. Bruwelheide, "Teacher Competencies For Microcomputer Use In The Classroom: A Literature Review," *Educational Technology* 22, no. 10 (1982): 29-30.
12. H. J. Becker, *IEA Computers.*
13. J. Bruwelheide, "Teacher Competencies," (1982): 29-30; N. Harrod and M. Ruggles, "Computer-Assisted Instruction: An Educational Tool," *Focus on Exceptional Children* 16, no. 1 (Sept. 1983):1-8.
14. E. O'Donnell, "Teacher Perceptions of Their Personal Computer Needs to Integrate Computers Into Their Classroom Instruction" (Ed. D. diss., University of Southern California, 1991).
15. H. J. Becker, *Instructional Uses of Microcomputers* (Baltimore, MD: The Johns Hopkins University Center for Social Organization of Schools, 1985).
16. Elmer-Dewitt, "The Revolution," 48-49.
17. Luning, B. "Integrating the Computer Into Classroom Instruction" (Ph. D. diss., Texas A & M University, 1985).
18. Office of Technology Assessment, *Power On!*
19. C. Ingersoll, C. Smith, and P. Elliott, "Microcomputers in American Public Schools: A National Survey," *Educational Computer* 3, no. 6 (1988): 28-31.
20. Becker, *IEA Computers*
21. J. D. Winkler, *Administrative Policies for Increasing the Use of Microcomputers in Instruction* (Santa Monica, CA: Rand Corporation, 1986): 3-73.
22. Ibid.
23. R. Main and L. Roberts "An Assessment of Educational Applications."
24. Ibid.
25. D. Moursund, "Microcomputers Will Not Solve the Computers-in-Education Problem," *AEDS Journal* 13, no. 1 (1979):31-39.
26. R. Robbat, "The Utilization of Computers in High School History Education" (Ph. D. diss. University of Oregon, 1984).
27. Ibid.
28. Ibid.
29. P. Stemmer and E. Carlson, "Addressing the Challenge of Training Competent Trainers in Computer Literacy" (paper

presented at the American Educational Research Association
meeting, ED 280 443, 1986:12.

30. Moursund, "Microcomputers."
31. C. Fawson and D. Van Uitert, "The Technology Enhanced
    Learning Environment" *Technology Trends for Readers in
    Education and Training* 35 (1990): 29-34
32. I. Bruder, "Restructuring Schools through Technology," *Business
    Week* (10 Dec. 1990): 32-38
33. D. Moursund, "Microcomputers."
34. Ibid.
35. C. Stasz, "Staff Development For Instructional Uses of Micro-
    computers: The Teachers' Perspective" (paper presented at
    meeting of American Educational Research Association, Santa
    Monica, CA: April 1984).
36. C. Stutzman, "Computer Supported Instruction in California
    Elementary and Secondary Schools: A Status Report," (paper
    presented at the Annual Research Symposium, Fresno, CA, April
    1981).

Chapter 2

NEED FOR QUALITY IN-SERVICE TRAINING PROGRAMS

There is a great deal of concern among educators about the classroom teacher's ability to utilize computers effectively in instruction. Lipkin found that over 90 percent of U. S. teachers lack computer skills.[1] Milner believes that 61 percent of teachers do not feel adequately prepared for classroom computer use.[2] Although these findings differ, there is clearly a need for in-service computer training. The California Technology Project (CTP), a statewide survey of California schools conducted by Main and Roberts, found that, as educational technology use increases, training becomes critical. The CTP report also states that staff development is a problem for almost one in three schools.[3] Lipkin believes that teachers should know how to incorporate the microcomputer into the subject matter or into aspects of the curriculum being taught.[4] Maddux states that the current level of computer training is too basic.[5] Kay found that teachers are entering the classroom without a great deal of computer skills or awareness or even a positive attitude toward computers.[6]

About one in every five schools reports plans to provide in-service training for teachers, administrators, or clerical staff.[7] Such training is necessary because, as noted by Main and Roberts, microcomputers are firmly embedded in American schools, with an average expenditure of $23,000 for microcomputers per school site.[8] Elmer-Dewitt found that currently computer hardware and software expenditures in American schools are estimated to be $1 billion a year.[9] Moreover, Main and Roberts found that 94 percent of schools reported plans to expand instructional use of microcomputers.[10] These schools also reported that they expected problems of content and delivery of in-service computer programs for teachers to become a major concern.

Bitter believes that educators must respond to society's need for computer literacy.[11] Bitter and Davis emphasize that teachers must be given opportunities to acquire computer skills and should be encouraged by administrators to do so.[12] The authors also state that teachers are insecure about their computer abilities and are eager to prepare themselves to use computers in their classroom instruction.[13]

In a 1982 Computers In Education survey, Becker found that of the 238 teachers surveyed, 72 percent of the respondents indicated a need for in-service training in computer use.[14] Darrow indicates that in-service training is a major factor in the success or failure of computer integration into the instructional process.[15] Stemmer and Carlson believe that adequately trained teachers are essential to the effective use of microcomputers in instruction.[16]

Lack of Knowledge Concerning In-Service Training

There is a serious lack of knowledge regarding what constitutes an effective staff development program for the integration of computers into the classroom. Currently there are no effective guidelines to follow for the in-service of teachers for computer integration in the classroom. School systems have employed many different models of staff development training in the absence of effective guidelines. Despite the lack of information on what leads to successful implementation of computers in instruction, school districts have made admirable strides in the instructional computer in-service of teachers. However, teachers are still not utilizing computers on a widespread basis.

In a study of 27 school districts in Wisconsin, Huther found no correlation between teacher use of computers in the classroom and in-service computer training.[17] In several studies of in-service computer training of teachers, Fullan found that the in-service computer training received was ineffective in promoting teacher change.[18]

Existing programs for teacher in-service for the integration of computers in the classroom are often inadequate and most often do not fulfill teacher needs. Robbat studied the use of computers by high school history teachers. In his sample of 51 teachers, only one teacher made use of computers in the instructional process, although approximately half of the teachers had received prior in-service computer training.[19]

Milner believes that there has been legitimate criticism directed at educational institutions because of computer misuse and ill-prepared or unqualified teachers using computers.[20] This criticism has led to many cases of teacher fear of computers or in some cases to a cessation of classroom computer use. It has become imperative that educators know what computer knowledge is useful to teachers in order to conduct effective in-service training for instructional computing.

Hoover states that the focus of computer staff development has changed over the last decade.[21] During the 1980s, the focus of teacher in-service training was on instructing teachers in the fundamentals of using and evaluating software, operating a computer, and programming. Currently, the emphasis is on teacher involvement and commitment. It is clear that neither researchers nor educators have reached a consensus on the specific proficiencies needed to integrate computers into the classroom.

Teacher Attitudes as Critical

As part of the Minnesota Educational Computing Consortium (MECC), Klassen directed a study in which he found that teacher training and attitudes toward computing are critical in determining teacher involvement in instructional computing.[22] Holmes also found that teacher acceptance and support are crucial to the implementation of computers and that without teacher support innovations will not be accepted by teachers.[23]

At the Merrimack Education Center, working with scores of school systems around the U.S. and through work with regional, state, and national education agencies, Mojkowski found that staff development needs for teachers and administrators are greatly underestimated. Moreover, Mojkowski believes that both the quality and the quantity of teacher training for instructional computer use deserve attention.[24]

Research shows that for the integration of computers into the curriculum, there are new behaviors that teachers must learn, which involve a high degree of change. Carey states that these new behavior patterns may cause anxiety and involve a great deal of frustration until teachers become thoroughly knowledgeable and comfortable with the innovation. Carey also believes that these new behaviors are learned over a period of time.[25] Teacher support and cooperation are necessary to the success of in-service training programs. School districts cannot assume that all teachers will immediately and enthusiastically embrace computers into their classroom instructional process, even after receiving in-service training.

Change and Innovation Research

The research on implementation of innovations in education emphasizes that the integration of computers into the classroom is a complex process with a multiplicity of factors. As a result, educators responsible for teacher in-service need to enlist teacher cooperation.

Researchers have found that programs of in-service that accommodate teachers' implementation decisions are more likely to fulfill the needs of the teachers and the district.[26] Berman and MacLaughlin found that teacher input was essential in gaining commitment to the innovation.[27] Teacher input into decision making is one of the primary enablers that will lead to successful in-service training of teachers. Without sincere acceptance and involvement of teachers in the planning and development process, teacher in-service for the integration of computers into the classroom is doomed to failure.

Fullan concluded that teacher characteristics, such as age and years of education, have little or no relation to successful implementation of innovations.[28] Researchers have found that implementation succeeds only when specific teacher needs are identified and clearly stated.[29] In addition, Beall and Harty found that a perception of confidence among teachers has a positive influence on their microcomputer implementation proneness.[30] Therefore, a positive climate in which to facilitate the inclusion of computer technology in teacher in-service education programs is necessary.[31]

A specific problem in the design and development of in-service programs that focus on the integration of computers in the classroom is that computers are threatening to many teachers, which results in a resistance to the change. Such resistance lessens involvement in the use of computers in the classroom.[32] Innovation research has emphasized the difficulty of conducting even planned change in education. Many educators have learned through experience that there is a need for teacher cooperation in order to facilitate computer integration into the classroom. A primary manner of enlisting teacher cooperation is to enlist teacher support through the total process of the design and the development of the computer in-service training program.

In support of this belief, Tracy indicates that the teacher's sense of involvement in the change process is a major influence on the level of curricular change.[33] Teachers must accept the change, they must have a vested interest in the change, they must feel that their needs are being addressed, and they must believe that they are important to the change. Teachers who wish to be involved in the in-service training must have opportunities to participate in the design and the development of in-service computer training.

Brumbaugh and Rawitsch recommend that teachers be involved in planning activities and information dissemination about computers.[34] An important principle of in-service is active and participatory decision making about in-service by the teachers involved. This active decision making should be evidenced in a shared responsibility involving teachers and administrators which allows teachers to become active as co-helpers and co-learners, rather than as passive recipients. Successful in-service must fulfill teacher classroom needs.

To date, no emphasis has been placed on the in-service need to survey teachers to identify their perceived needs for actual classroom computer activities and competencies. Teachers become the learners, and as the learners and the recipients of the training, their needs must be specifically addressed. Being involved in the training is the first step. An identification of the specific teacher/learner needs is the second step to successful in-service training for computer integration in the classroom.

Principals and other administrators often make the decisions concerning the implementation of computers without consulting teachers. Meyer, however, has found that teacher participation in decision making concerning in-service training is necessary for successful implementation of all phases of computer programs.[35] In addition, Alonzo, Furth, and Neville believe that the people who participate in the change program should be involved in the planning and decision-making process.[36] A study by the Rand Corporation emphasizes that there is a significant relationship between teacher participation in decision making and effective implementation and continued use of the implementation.[37] The Rand study also found that when project objectives and activities reflected teacher input, the staff was more likely to invest the energy and interest needed to make the project work.

Bentzen, Goodland, and Hall have documented the importance of the role of the individual teacher in the change process.[38] The work of Cicchelli and Baeker emphasizes a personal approach to in-service programs focusing on the needs and concerns of individuals who are undergoing the change.[39] In order to facilitate the integration of computers in the classroom, Cicchelli and Baecher believe that staff development should focus on a personalized program that is responsive to the concerns of teachers.

Research has supported the belief that the integration of computers into the classroom is a complex process that is dependent upon the individual teacher and the amount of the teacher's resistance to change. Hall has verified that teacher acceptance of change is of paramount importance to the successful implementation of that change. Hall identifies the major reason for the failure to implement an innovation as the lack of attention given to the individual teacher involved in the change process.[40] However, teacher involvement alone will not lead to successful in-service training. It is the quality of the involvement, and the specific identification of actual teacher needs that have the power to prove successful. Too often administrators involve teachers in the development phases of in-service training while reserving the very important initial planning decisions, such as budget expenditures and the design of the in-service training, for themselves. Often these very important decisions are made before teachers are invited to join the process.

In the past, the authoritarian behavior of administrators has hindered teacher participation in implementing educational computer use. The current practice is to implement integration of micro-computers into the classroom with the cooperation of supportive principals who enlist the services of a highly skilled computer teacher or a computer coordinator, whom the principals believe classroom teachers view as a peer, in an effort to gain teacher support and cooperation. This computer coordinator is not an administrator or a classroom teacher, but is rather an agent of change, who in reality is not seen by teachers as a peer. Any authoritarian position is disempowering for teachers and should be guarded against.

Humanistic Psychology

An important orientation from humanistic psychology, which is highly useful for educators when integrating computers into the classroom, is that teachers need to take a personal interest in the identification and formulation of the goals. Inherent in the humanistic psychology approach to the integration of computers into the classroom is the recognition of teacher needs, involving teachers in a meaningful manner in the decision-making process, and fostering a supportive, non-threatening environment. Brunner believes also that computers and technologies will remain unused to full capacity until the classroom teacher is allowed to become fully involved in the planning and implementation of computers into the curriculum.[41]

In studies on feedback, it has been found that if educational technologists or change agents function in a judgmental manner, their views are likely to be rejected by the majority of teachers.[42] The research clearly indicates that educational technologists as well as administrators should function in a highly supportive manner.

In-Service Training and the Culture of Teaching

Aquila and Parrish believe that the initial teacher rejection of computers in the classroom may be due to teacher fear and a general mistrust of administrative decisions. They strongly believe that a new approach is needed for staff development that emphasizes teacher professionalism, respect, and dignity.[43]

Aquila and Parrish believe that any school change is a cultural change.[44] They state that two distinct types of culture can be found in schools, the craft culture and the technical culture, and often these two factions are seen as opposing factors, with teachers as craft culture and administrators and change agents as technical culture.[45]

It is thought that technical cultures readily accept technical innovations while craft cultures do not. Thus, it would appear that for successful implementation of computers into the classroom, it is necessary to understand the craft culture of teaching. Researchers state that educators believe that when teachers understand an innovation and when there is implementation assistance and something to implement, they will do so. However, this is a mistaken assumption without foundation in either research or experience.[46]

It has become clear that educators need to consider a wide variety of teacher characteristics concerning the acceptance of computers into the classroom. The needs of the the craft culture must be taken into consideration by educators responsible for the in-service training of teachers to integrate computers into the curriculum. An identification of the unique characteristics of teachers of the craft culture will allow recognition of these specific needs. However, all teachers possess unique and varying competencies, as their students do. For successful integration of computers into the classroom, all teacher needs must be met.

To date, very few studies that focus on the importance of teacher self-perceived needs have been undertaken. Humanistic psychology research points to the importance of the interpersonal relationships between teachers and administrators or change agents when designing in-service programs to integrate computers into the classroom. Although researchers agree that staff development for computer implementation should be the primary focus of instructional computer use and that teachers must be cooperative and supportive for successful integration, very few studies have focused the attention on classroom teacher self-perceived needs. Yet research strongly indicates that efforts to bring about change in the schools should be more responsive to the needs of the classroom teacher.

Teacher Studies of Perceived Needs for Computer In-Service

There are no studies that asked a broad spectrum of classroom teachers what their specific needs are for integrating computers into the classroom. Schmid surveyed classroom teachers of social science about whether they thought computers were readily available to them and how they might use them in the classroom.[47] The goal of this study was to enhance dialogue between programmers and K-12 instructors; it did not gather data on teacher perceived needs.

Under the direction of Sheingold and Hadley, the Center for Technology in Education conducted a national survey of 1,200 teachers.[48] These teachers were chosen for the survey for their accomplishments in integrating computers into their classroom curriculum. They are not a cross section of all teachers; rather, they are a special group recognized for their computer accomplishments. The results of this survey show that these teachers had required approximately five to six years, on the average, to master computer-based approaches to classroom teaching and that the process of change was slow, even with a special group of teachers who readily accepted technology. Sheingold and Hadley are skeptical that the process of integrating computers into the classroom can happen quickly.[49]

Bitter and Davis surveyed 240 teachers who were computer education students at Arizona State University. The results revealed a positive correlation between attitudes toward computers and the level of computer knowledge of the respondents.[50] This study also was not conducted with average classroom teachers. As noted, the participants of this survey were enrolled in computer classes at the university.

The only study that surveyed typical classroom teachers was the Schmid study of social science teachers, discussed above.[51] The other studies were surveys of special groups of teachers, such as the Bitter and Davis and the Sheingold and Hadley studies.[52] This type of research, of surveying special groups, offers valuable information for the integration of computers into the curriculum. However, it is necessary to move from special groups who have readily accepted computers into their classroom to the general body of classroom teachers that form the craft culture of teaching. As Aquila and Parrish have shown, it is highly likely that if teachers have readily embraced computers into their classroom instruction, they are not representative of the large cadre of classroom teachers who make up the craft culture of teaching, but are representative of a technical culture.[53]

Although many researchers agree that staff development for microcomputer implementation is important, there is no consensus regarding the competencies needed by teachers for successful microcomputer implementation. Researchers see a definite need for teachers to become computer proficient, but these same researchers differ on what constitutes successful staff development programs. There seems to be no research upon which educators can rely regarding the structure of in-service training programs. Therefore, it makes sense to ask teachers who are to participate in the training what they perceive their computer needs to be.

Relationship between Lack of Classroom Computer Use by Teachers and In-Service Projects

Many studies on computer use by teachers indicate that, although computers are widespread in schools, their use by classroom teachers is not widespread. A recent survey by Rheinhold and Corkett showed that every state in the U.S. is actively training teachers for classroom computer use.[54] Kinnaman found that over half the states require or recommend technology training.[55] Stemmer and Carlson believe that the growth of microcomputer use in schools is so rapid that there must be a response to the teachers' need for training.[56] Studies on the implementation of innovations are unanimous in their conclusions that effective implementation is more likely to succeed in schools where opportunities for teacher participation in the planning process are plentiful.[57]

At present, however, there is no consensus regarding the content of in-service programs or the competencies needed by teachers for successful classroom computer integration.[58] Although a large number of research studies have identified successful aspects of computer training, only O'Donnell went directly to large numbers of classroom teachers and asked them to identify their own needs for computer training.[59]

In view of the research that computers in schools are not being utilized by the majority of teachers and school districts are expending significant amounts of funds on computers and staff training, it becomes even more important to recognize that the present in-service programs do not guarantee any change in teacher behavior.

The O'Donnell study addressed this issue by going directly to classroom teachers and asking them about their self-perceived needs for the integration of computers into their classroom curriculum. Moreover, the study assessed classroom teachers' perceived needs for specific strategies to integrate computers into their classroom instruction, and also assessed the areas of computer skills in which they would like to receive additional training.[60]

Notes

1. J. Lipkin, "A Teacher and a Place," *Education Times* 1, no.7 (1982): 7-9.
2. S. Milner, "Teaching Teachers About Computers: A Necessity for Education," *Phi Delta Kappan* 61, no. 8 (1990): 544-46.
3. R. Main and L. Roberts, "An Assessment of Educational Applications," *California Technology Project Quarterly* 1, no. 2 (1990): 17.
4. J. Lipkin, "A Teacher and a Place."
5. C. Maddux, "Scientific Dedication or Religious Fanaticism in the 1980s," *Educational Technology* 29, no. 2 (1989): 18-23.
6. R. Kay, "Predicting Student Teacher Commitment to the Use of Computers," *Journal of Educational Computing Research* 6, no. 3 (1990): 299-309.
7. Main and Roberts, "An Assessment of Educational Applications," 17.
8. Ibid.
9. P. Elmer-Dewitt, "The Revolution That Fizzled" *Time* (May, 1991), 48-49.
10. Main and Roberts, "An Assessment of Educational Applications."

11. G. Bitter, *Computers in Today's World* (New York: Wiley, 1984).
12. G. Bitter and S. Davis, "Measuring the Development of Computer Literacy among Teachers" *AEDS Journal* 18, no.4 (1985): 243-45.
13. Ibid.
14. H. J. Becker, *School Uses of Microcomputers* 2 (Baltimore, MD: The Johns Hopkins University, Center For Social Organization of Schools, 1982): 3.
15. M. Darrow, *Computer Alliance Fact Sheet: Consumer Tips for School Districts on Microcomputer Hardware and Software* (Alexandria, VA: National School Boards Association, 1984): 3.
16. P. Stemmer, and E. Carlson, "Addressing the Challenge of Training Competent Trainers in Computer Literacy" (paper presented at the American Educational Research Association April meeting, 1986, ERIC: ED 280 443).
17. P. Huther, "Factors Associated With the Extent of Microcomputer Curriculum Implementation in K-12 School Systems" (Ph. D. diss., University of Wisconsin, 1984) abstract in *Dissertation Abstracts International* 45 (1984): 1939A.
18. M. Fullan, *The Meaning of Educational Change* (New York: Teachers College Press, 1987): 53-54.
19. R. Robbat, "The Utilization of Computers in High School History Education" (Ph.D. diss., University of Oregon, 1984): 2.
20. S. Milner, "Teaching Teachers," 544-46.
21. T. Hoover, "The Changing Focus of In-Service for Educational Computers," *Educational Computer* (Nov/Dec. 1982): 36-37.
22. P. Klassen, *A Study of Computer Use and Literacy in Science Education: A Final Report* (St. Paul, MN: Minnesota Educational Computer Consortium, 1980).
23. G. Holmes, "Computer-Assisted Instruction: A Discussion of Some of the Issues for Would-Be Implementers," *Educational Technology* 22, no. 9 (1982): 7-13.
24. C. Mojkowski, "10 Essential Truths to Help You Plan for Technology," *Technology Trends* 30, no. 7 (1985): 18-21.
25. D. Carey, "An Investigation of Factors That Effect Elementary School Teachers: Educational Use of Computers" (Ph. D. diss., University of Oregon, 1985).
26. R. Elmore, *Complexity and Control: What Legislators and Administrators Can Do about Implementing Public Policy* (Washington, DC: National Institute for Education, 1980); W.

Williams, *The Implementation Perspective* (Berkeley: University of California Press, 1980).

27. P. Berman and M. MacLaughlin, *An Explanatory Study of School District Adaptations* (Santa Monica, CA: Rand Corporation, 1978): 3-50.
28. M. Fullan, *The Meaning of Educational Change*, 53-4.
29. J. Emrich and S. Peterson, *A Synthesis of Findings across Five Recent Studies in Educational Dissemination and Change* (San Francisco, CA: Far West Laboratories, 1978); K. Louis and S. Sieber, *Bureaucracy and the Dispersed Organization* (Norwood, NJ: Ablex, 1979).
30. D. Beall and H. Harty, "Inservice Teacher Reactions to Implementing Microcomputers in Elementary Science and Mathematics Classes," *The Journal of Computers in Mathematics and Science Teaching* 3, no. 4 (1980): 34-48.
31. D. Stevens, "Microcomputers: An Educational Challenge" *Computers and Education* 8, no. 2 (1984): 263-67.
32. L. Cady, *Computer Technology in Curriculum and Instruction Handbook: Design for Staff Development* (Olympia, Washington Office of the State Superintendent of Public Instruction, 1982).
33. P. Tracy, *High Tech, Low Tech, and Education* (Dearborn, MI: University, 1986).
34. K. Brumbaugh and D. Rawitsch, *Establishing Instructional Computing: The First Steps* (St. Paul: Minnesota Computer Consortium, 1982).
35. J. Meyer, "What Classroom Teachers Would Love to Tell Administrators about Computers or How to Successfully Introduce Computers into Your School District's Curriculum" (paper presented at Annual Conference of the Educational Computing Consortium of Ohio. ERIC Document: ED 266 772, 1985).
36. R. Alonzo, G. Furth, and R. Neville, *Instructional Supervision: A Behavioral System* (Boston: Allyn and Bacon, 1981).
37. J. Winkler, *The Rand Study: Administrative Policies for Increasing the Use of Microcomputers in Instruction* (Santa Monica, CA: The Rand Corporation, 1987): 3-73.
38. N. Bentzen, *Changing Schools: The Magic Feature Principle* (New York: McGraw-Hill,1981); J. Goodland, *Behind the Classroom Door* (Worthington, OH: Wadsworth, 1980); G. Hall, "Teacher Concerns as a Basis for Facilitating and Personalizing

Staff Development," *Teacher College,* report 1, no. 80 (1981): 36-53.

39. T. Cicchelli, and R. Baecher, "The Use of Concerns Theory in In-service Training for Computer Education," *Computer Education* 11, no. 2 (1987): 85-93.
40. Hall, "Teacher Concerns," 36-53.
41. C. Brunner, "What It Really Means to Integrate Technology," *Technology and Learning* 11, no. 3 (1990): 12-14.
42. S. Brown, G. Kirkup, R. Melton, and E. Scanlon, "Checklist for Evaluation of Teaching at a Distance *Institutional Research Review* 2 (1983): 15-58. R. Melton and R. Zimmer, "Multiperspective Illumination," *British Journal of Educational Technology* 18, no. 2 (1986): 111-20.
43. F. Aquila and R. Parrish, "The Clash of Cultures: Instructional Technology and the Craft of Teaching," *Journal of Research and Development in Education* 22, (1989): 49-55.
44. Ibid.
45. Ibid.
46. D. Crandall and S. Loucks, *A Study of Dissemination Efforts Supporting School Improvement* (Landover, MD: Network, 1987; Aquila and Parrish, "The Clash of Cultures," 49-55; J. Sarason, *The Culture of the School and the Problem of Change* (Boston: Allyn and Bacon, 1971).
47. J. Schmid, "Survey of Computer Use in Missouri Social Science Classrooms Reveals Problems and Promise," *The Journal: Technological Horizons in Education* 18, no. 3 (1990): 86-9.
48. K. Sheingold and M. Hadley, *Accomplished Teachers: Integrating Computers Into Classroom Practice* (New York: Center for Technology in Education, Bank Street College of Education, 1990).
49. Ibid.
50. G. Bitter and S. Davis, "Measuring the Development," 243-53.
51. Aquila and Parrish, "The Clash of Cultures," 40-55.
52. Bitter and Davis, "Measuring the Development," 243-53; Sheingold and Hadley, *Accomplished Teachers,* 30-31.
53. G. Aquila and Parrish, "The Clash of Cultures," 49-55.
54. F. Rheinhold and K. Corkett, "Mandates: Yes, No, Maybe: Electronic Learning's Fifth Annual Survey of the States," *Electronic Learning* 5, no. 2 (1985): 25-31.

55. D. Kinnaman, "What's the Research Telling Us?" *Classroom Computer Learning* 10, no. 6 (1990): 31-35.
56. Stemmer and Carlson, "Addressing the Challenge," 3-5.
57. Berman and MacLaughlin, *An Explanatory Study*, 23-5; S. Rosenblum and K. Louis, *Stability and Change: Innovation in an Educational Context* (Cambridge, MA: ABT, 1979).
58. J. Bruwelheide, "Teacher Competencies for Microcomputer Use in the Classroom: A Literature Review," *Educational Technology* 22, no. 10 (1982): 29-30.
59. E. O'Donnell, "Teacher Perceptions of Their Personal Computer Needs to Integrate Computers into Their Classroom Instruction" (Ed. D. diss., The University of Southern California, 1991).
60. Ibid.

Chapter 3

A NEW PATTERN OF IN-SERVICE TRAINING

This book identifies some of the systemic problems with current preservice and in-service staff development programs. Suggestions are offered for implementing instructional computer training programs in a cost-effective manner, while avoiding ineffective preservice and in-service staff development programs. The following chapters also provide a guide from which school and district administrators can design and develop successful in-service computer training for teachers. These frameworks offer the keys to successful computer integration into classroom instruction. The frameworks and guidelines contained in this book enable the total integration of computers into the instructional process from kindergarten through twelfth grade, in a cost-effective and facile manner.

Chapters 5-8 offer practical guidelines for each level of education, school district administrators, and university faculties when planning, developing, and implementing staff development training programs. In addition, current research findings must drive the design process of the programs. There must be cooperation between all levels of education to successfully address planning and implementation of effective staff development programs that offer teachers the necessary skills to integrate computers into classrooms.

Chapters 9-13 of this book provide an organized schema or guide that coordinates teacher staff development training at all levels: school site, school district, and the university. Chapter 14 calls for national standards to be developed for computer integration into the classroom. The process of integrating computers into the daily classroom is complex and involves a multiplicity of factors that require cooperation and articulation between all levels of education.

The following guidelines for designing staff development programs are purposefully written in a general manner that allows adaptation to the individual needs of each school district or educational situation. These plans should be consistent with existing practices of the district and with teacher talents and skills. The frameworks that follow are based upon research that specifically identifies sensitive areas in which exemplary staff development practices have proven to be successful. In addition, these guidelines focus on teacher needs for computer integration which have been identified by research. By utilizing strategic planning, as these guidelines emphasize, the specific needs of teachers are addressed in a cost-effective manner. Strategic planning builds a strong foundation on which to identify and meet the computer needs of teachers while developing successful staff development programs. Strategic planning based upon the specific needs of teachers is the key to developing computer in-service programs that are effective and enthusiastically received. District-wide strategic planning is the most important component for setting a direction for the instructional use of computers and targeting the specific needs of teachers.

The focus of this book is to offer guidelines, based upon the findings of the O'Donnell survey, which school districts can use. These guidelines should be combined with on-site strategic planning to fully and effectively integrate computers into the classroom curriculum.[1] The guidelines also provide frameworks for school districts and colleges of education to follow when designing staff-development programs to integrate computers into the classroom.

A New Philosophy

Past staff development programs have not focused on the specific instructional computer skills needed by teachers to integrate computers into classrooms. Currently staff development programs are designed to offer hands-on skills that do not provide teachers with the instructional strategies and pedagogical methods necessary to integrate computers into classroom instruction. As a result, teachers who are sincere about utilizing technology in their classrooms have had to seek out their own training to go beyond hands-on skills. However, many teachers do not have the time to do so. To achieve successful in-service, the basic philosophy that has driven staff development efforts in the past must be changed.

A new philosophy must recognize that just placing computers into classrooms is not adequate for computer integration.Such a philosophy also must recognize that teachers wish to integrate computers into instruction but do not know how. Finally, a recognition that present in-service programs are inadequate for widespread integration of computers into the classroom is necessary. Stasz and Shavelson contend that the integration of computers with subject matter and classroom activities is the least well-addressed issue in staff development sessions.[2]

In-service training must not only address hands-on skills, but must go appreciably further to offer teachers the student-centered computer techniques and instructional strategies required to integrate computers into the classroom. Training must meet teacher needs by offering whole class instructional methods that can be easily integrated into the classroom curriculum. Teachers must gain the necessary instructional strategies to go beyond hands-on computer skills to teacher-driven instructional strategies that provide confidence and enthusiasm to inspire utilization of computers in a whole class environment.

School Districts Are Not Prepared

Currently, most school districts do not have sufficient funds or experienced personnel to design, develop, and implement effective staff development programs. The guidelines in this book emphasize that existing staff can be utilized, with the addition of a professional instructional design technologist. At present, many school districts do not employ an instructional design technologist on staff, but rely on resource teachers for curriculum design. A major component of this plan requires that a professional instructional design technologist be added to the permanent staff.

The duties of the instructional design technologist encompass the development and the implementation of appropriate staff development training programs for the integration of computers into the classroom. These duties include the design of instructional materials to facilitate the integration of computers. In addition, a major responsibility of the instructional design technologist is to provide sustained assistance for classroom teachers as they integrate computers into the classroom curriculum.

Brief In-Service Training Sessions

In the past the norm has been to conduct brief training sessions that offer only awareness and hands-on keyboarding skills, utilizing staff personnel who are themselves unskilled in staff development techniques to conduct the training sessions. Therefore, teachers must rely on inexperienced personnel who do not have the appropriate background or the necessary professional experience to design and implement effective staff development programs for instructional computing. Who has not attended sessions where the information offered was not applicable to a whole class environment or where the technical equipment that was being demonstrated did not work? This is an irreparable situation in computer staff development training sessions. It does not offer teachers the necessary skills to integrate computers into the classroom and it sends the message that computers are difficult to operate. Teachers will not accept the possibility of seeming incompetent in front of their classes.

Many school districts have contracted with county offices or outside consultants when designing staff development programs. This also has not proven successful, because again, the basic issue of addressing teachers' unique needs has not been addressed. Most school districts are unaware of teachers' specific needs to integrate computers into the classroom. Outside agencies are not familiar with teacher patterns unless the school district has communicated this information to the providing agency. The unique needs of teachers must be the focus of each staff development session. In addition, repetition and time are required to effect lasting change in classroom instructional methods. Staff development must cover an ongoing period of time with sustained, consistent follow-up assistance for teachers.

Craft Culture of Teaching

A Dell Company computer study reported that fear of technology may be the fear of the 1990s, with 55 percent of Americans considered to be technophobic.[3] The fear of computers is very real, similar to the fears experienced when starting a new job or learning to drive a car. The Dell study also found that teenagers are more computer literate than adults and that many teachers tend to be fearful of computers and will not use a computer unless forced to do so. Teachers of the craft culture view teaching as a fine art rather than a technical skill and are often hesitant to accept computers in the classroom. The majority of teachers of the craft culture are afraid that they are unable to operate a computer successfully and will not only look foolish in the classroom but will be labeled incompetent.

There is a very real basis for the fears that teachers of the craft culture experience. This must be recognized when conducting staff development training sessions. Teachers of the craft culture require more supportive in-service computer training than teachers of the technical culture. Teachers who exhibit seemingly uncooperative behavior toward in-service sessions are often driven by fear.

Teachers of the technical culture are quicker to perceive the benefits of computers in the classroom than are teachers of the craft culture. Teachers of the craft culture may resist computers because they perceive computers to be difficult to operate and as increasing their work load and their classroom preparation time. It is usually a teacher of the technical culture who will invest the time, effort, and funds into achieving the education and skills that lead to integration of computers into the classroom. Teachers of the craft culture may not wish to spend the time, effort, and funds necessary to attain computer competency. A teacher's fear of computers cannot be expected to be alleviated in one or two brief in-service training sessions.

Wholistic View of Computer In-Service Training

One endemic problem with computer integration programs is that there are no long-range plans. Many districts have developed in-service plans that extend from one to three years. However, research has clearly shown that it takes approximately five to six years to develop the computer competency needed to integrate computers into the classroom successfully.[4] Research also has shown that only long-range planning can lead to successful computer integration into the classroom. With the severe budget deficits that school districts face, staff-development training is currently under-funded and without long-range, well-organized plans or the personnel on staff to implement the plan. It takes time, practice, and specific instructional strategies that teachers are not familiar with to integrate computers into the classroom.

Integration is different from incorporating computers into a classroom within traditional teaching practices. *Integration* means to complete or to merge parts into a whole. To integrate computers into the classroom means to renew the whole and to supply the missing part that completes the whole. It means to heal the classroom in a holistic manner that is complete unto itself with all parts performing in perfect synchronicity. The goal of all computer in-service sessions should be to train teachers to integrate computers into a whole class environment, thereby attaining a wholistic classroom.

Computers must be utilized in ways that move from the tradition of individual students working in an isolated manner with drill and practice programs and rote tutorials into one that involves the teacher, the computer, and the whole class in interactive learning. This is computer integration in a wholistic manner that involves all aspects of classroom dynamics.

The philosophy of the past has been to incorporate computers into classrooms without changing basic classroom activities and without making the classroom whole. This, however, has not proved to be a valid approach. Computer in-service training programs must offer teachers the pedagogical techniques merged with hands-on skills necessary to go beyond the incorporation of computers into traditional instruction. Past computer in-service training programs have not offered the pedagogical techniques nor the instructional strategies that teachers require to utilize with computers to make their classrooms whole.

Incorporating computers into the classroom does not necessarily lead to the integration of computers into instruction. It may lead, however, to teacher disillusionment with computers, because the pedagogical task of integrating computers into traditional instruction becomes overwhelming without a knowledge of appropriate teacher-directed techniques merged with computer skills. It is virtually impossible for teachers to integrate computers into instruction with hands-on skills only. Therefore, continuing with the same pattern of preservice and in-service training becomes self-defeating. The vast majority of teachers have had no instructional strategies training and have no knowledge of the necessary pedagogical techniques to integrate computers into the curriculum.

Teachers must be trained away from teaching methods that invite only the traditional uses of classroom computers, such as drill and practice and tutorials. They must learn instructional strategies and classroom techniques that invite computer integration into the classroom curriculum. Research has shown that the very nature of teaching is altered with the integration of computers into the classroom.[5] Only time and teacher-focused staff development programs that address the retraining of teachers on a sustained basis will lead to successful integration of computers.

Change is necessarily a slow process because, before altering teaching practices, and beliefs must be altered.[6] Cultural norms and many school administrators continue to support traditional instruction.

Teachers must be offered pedagogical techniques that do not continue to support traditional instructional methods. It takes time, not only to replace traditional methods with appropriate instructional strategies, but also to demonstrate that this has taken place. Therefore, long-range computer in-service planning is necessary.

Notes

1. E. O'Donnell, "Teacher Perceptions of Their Personal Computer Needs to Integrate Computers Into Their Classroom Instruction." (Ed. D. diss., University of Southern California, 1991).
2. C. Stasz and R. Shavelson, "Staff Development for Instructional Uses of Microcomputers," *AEDS Journal* 19, no. 1 (1988): 1-19.
3. *NEWS* section, *Orange County Register* (27 July 1993): 9.
4. K. Sheingold and M. Hadley, *Accomplished Teachers: Integrating Computers into Classroom Practice* (New York: Center for Technology in Education, Bank Street College of Education, 1990).
5. C. Dwyer, C. Ringstaff, and J. Sandholtz, *Teacher Beliefs and Practices. Part II: Support for Change: The Evolution of Teachers' Instructional Beliefs and Practices in High-Access-To-Technology Classrooms, First to Fourth Year Findings,* ACOT report no. 9 (Apple Classrooms of Tomorrow: Advanced Technology Group, Apple Computer, Inc., 1990): 17.
6. Ibid.

Chapter 4

A WHOLISTIC VIEW OF IN-SERVICE TRAINING

The premise of this book is that current computer in-service efforts must change significantly if computers are to be integrated within the classrooms of American schools. Nothing less than a revolutionary restructuring of present procedures is necessary to achieve the goal of computer integration into the classroom. The lack of computer use by teachers can be attributed in large part to current and past staff development efforts that are based primarily on the hands-on aspects of training within traditional parameters.

Collis found that teachers who effectively utilize computers in classroom instruction differ only from teachers who do not by the length of training and experience they have had with computers.[1] Bitter and Davis found a positive correlation between computer attitudes and the level of knowledge about computers.[2] This research could be interpreted to imply that more experience and better training will lead to a positive attitude toward computers in the classroom. Despite a desire to use computers effectively in their classroom, most teachers have not received the sufficient or the appropriate training that they need to confidently and successfully integrate computers into instruction.

Hands-on training gives teachers the necessary skills to work with computers, but it does not give them the instructional strategies necessary to work with computers in the student-centered situations that are encountered in the classroom. In a recent study of elementary teachers in the state of Oregon, Lamon found that the number-one concern among teachers was a need for additional training for instructional computer uses.[3] In a series of teacher interviews, Wiske and Zodiates found that the lack of student-centered strategies for the use of computers in the classroom is significant and should not be discounted by administrators who are conducting staff development programs.[4]

While the need for introductory workshops is significant, more and more teachers who are entering service are familiar with computers and possess hands-on skills and an awareness of computers in the classroom. A knowledge of the relationships of students, teachers, and computers in the classroom and the teaching strategies necessary for successful computer integration into the classroom is becoming apparent among researchers. The linkages between effective computer use and effective classroom instruction must be the focus of computer preservice and in-service training.

The word *wholistic* is used in this book to describe an understanding of the utilization of computer integration in a whole class setting. Teachers must acquire a wholistic view of computer integration that encompasses a whole class setting, with appropriate classroom techniques and student-centered strategies that lead to computer integration, not computer incorporation within the traditional classroom. The wholistic view of staff development requires a structured, organized, and strategically planned approach to computer in-service training that encompasses a whole class setting. This approach is not evident in the majority of current instructional computer staff development programs.

The integration of computers into a whole class setting does not happen quickly; it happens slowly. Change cannot be imposed from without through external prodding or coercion. Change must come from within, through gentle assistance and subtle direction toward a predetermined goal. Change only happens when the external circumstances have framed the correct mental attitude to recognize that the change is beneficial for the teacher and the students. Integration of computers into the classroom necessitates a series of events that are directed toward the factors which are prohibiting the successful integration of computers into the classroom. These events must shift teacher beliefs and classroom dynamics from the instructional methods of the past to teaching methods that will facilitate the integration of computers into the instructional process.

Classroom Dynamics

Computer integration into the classroom cannot be discussed seriously without considering the role of the classroom teacher. The teacher makes the critical decisions concerning classroom dynamics that decide the future of computer integration into the classroom on a widespread basis. Currently, classroom dynamics usually involve one teacher working with students in a self-contained classroom with a classic lecture format. It remains for the teacher alone to manage instruction and classroom dynamics appropriately for the integration of computers. How well the teacher is able to work with computers within whole class instruction is currently dependent upon the personal effort of the teacher.

Within whole class dynamics, the instructional computer response of teachers is directly related to the level of computer use and the knowledge of appropriate instructional strategies to employ with computer use in the classroom. Without confidence in their abilities to utilize computers successfully in the classroom, teachers are hesitant to accept computers as an instructional tool. Many teachers are concerned about their ability to utilize computers effectively and therefore have questions concerning the efficacy of computers within classroom dynamics.

Effective instructional computer use greatly changes the nature of the classroom environment. However, in the early stages of computer use, teaching methods remain virtually the same. Initially teachers utilize computers within traditional instruction without modifying pedagogical methods or student-centered classroom strategies.[5] The utilization of computers in this manner allows classroom dynamics to remain static; however, this type of computer use does not allow teachers to realize the full potential of computers as an instructional tool in a whole class setting.

Efficacy of Computers in Instruction

It is evident that computers are significantly changing our educational system. However, it is not readily apparent how computers are affecting achievement.[6] Research has attempted to identify the specific ways that instructional computing has affected learning, but, much work remains to be done. It is generally accepted that computers will heighten initial enthusiasm of teachers and students.[7] However, once the novelty effect lessens, computers are often overlooked as an instructional asset.[8]

The efficacy of computer integration is a concern of teachers.[9] At the present time, there are no real answers concerning efficacy. The results of research are often confusing and conflicting.[10] Many of the positive results are preceded by such descriptors as "potentially" or "usually." For example, Roblyer analyzed studies done between 1980 and 1987 to provide information concerning the efficacy of computers in instruction. His meta-analysis found that using computer applications seems to improve student attitudes toward school and subject matter.[11] However, the existing data are insufficient to indicate whether better attitudes have any impact on academic achievement or on dropout rate.[12]

Kulik found that although certain aspects of computer-based instruction are still unclear, some research findings are definite. In two meta-analysis reviews of instructional computing studies, Kulik states that the effectiveness of computer-assisted instruction may be limited by its use as a complete replacement for conventional instruction.[13] In 1987, Kulik again utilized meta-analysis, this time to review four symposium papers that brought together 199 comparative studies. Kulik found that students generally learned more in classes where CBI was used, learned their lessons in less time, liked classes more, and developed a more positive attitude. However, computer instruction had little effect on course withdrawal and attitude toward subject matter. Interestingly, Kulik suggested that editorial screening, experimental design flaws, and instructional quality, rather than the efficacy of computers, may have contributed to this favorable picture of CBI.[14]

Hawley found no significant differences between mathematics instruction of students with computers and those who did not use computers.[15] Schlechter found that questions remain concerning the educational value of small group computer-assisted instruction. No consistent effects were found on achievement or retention scores when computers were used with either small groups or with individual instruction.[16] Cosden found that teacher perceptions of the effectiveness of computers in instruction was in the motivational, not the academic, realm.[17] Clark found that there is often confounding in computer-based instructional studies.[18]

As teachers become aware of the conflicting results of computer studies, many are discouraged. The craft culture seems to be hesitant to accept a technical change. When teachers begin to ask questions concerning the efficacy of computers, they tend to assess and to evaluate the available information in terms of their classrooms. Teachers will resist or support instructional computer use based upon their individual beliefs concerning the instructional possibilities of computers.

Teachers must perceive the value of the computer's efficacy in the classroom before they invest time, effort, and funds gaining the complex skills necessary for the integration of computers into the instructional process. Many teachers have not acquired the sophisticated instructional computing skills that lead to classroom computer integration. Therefore, they do not realize the rewards of effective instructional computer use.

The studies on the integration of computers into the classroom have, for the most part, ignored the teacher.[19] This is a major reason why studies on computer effectiveness have shown varying, confusing, and conflicting results.[20] Teacher effects have not been studied. When computers are incorporated but not fully integrated into instruction, results will be varying and confounded. The teacher is pivotal to the classroom integration of computers.[21] As teachers become more confident in their computer abilities, computer effectiveness in the classroom can be studied in a more successful manner.

Computer Empowerment

Despite the strong advances in instructional computing during the last decade, the level of instructional computing among the majority of teachers has remained at the awareness or the hands-on level. However, these are not the skills necessary to integrate computers into instruction. Hands-on skills offer teachers only an awareness of computers that leads to incorporation of computers into instruction, not the integration of computers into instruction. O'Donnell found that teachers desire training in instructional strategies and pedagogical methods necessary to integrate computers into classroom instruction.[22] Instructional computer training must offer teachers the pedagogical skills necessary to comfortably and confidently integrate computers into instruction.

Computer empowerment for teachers must be nurtured by administrators if computers are to be fully integrated into classroom instruction. The necessary instructional strategies and pedagogical methods required by teachers to integrate computers into the classroom are the requisites for computer empowerment required by teachers. An assessment of specific teacher preservice and in-service instructional computer needs and staff development training to achieve those needs are vital to the success of classroom computer integration.

With computer empowerment, there also must be an effort to facilitate the acquisition of effective and continuing appropriate professional development for all teachers. The knowledge of instructional strategies interfaced with computer skills is the true empowerment that teachers require to confidently and successfully integrate computers into the classroom. With confidence in their computer abilities, teachers become empowered to integrate computers into the classroom. Computer empowerment leads to a wholistic classroom in which computers are utilized as a component of the classroom curriculum.

In the past, school administrators believed that a few computing teachers could serve as exemplary role models, mentors, and computer consultants to train and support their colleagues. This approach has served to introduce many teachers to computers; however, the task is much larger than anticipated. Administrators also mistakenly believed that teachers of the 1990s would enter the teaching profession with the appropriate skills to integrate computers into classrooms. Unfortunately, this has not proved to be true. Most districts have made valiant efforts to in-service teachers. However, school districts do not have the time or the resources to effectively train teachers to integrate computers into the classroom.

A paradigm of cooperation between colleges and school districts will prevent duplication of effort, be cost-effective, and offer teachers a higher quality of training. Computer integration training of teachers should be a joint effort between colleges of education and school districts.[23] School districts working alone do not have sufficient time, funds, or professional staff to conduct effective in-service instructional computer training programs. The cooperative framing of guidelines between school districts and colleges of education will allow both to offer the specific training that teachers require for widespread integration of computers into the classroom.

Notes

1. B. Collis, *The Best of Research Windows: Trends and Issues in Educational Computing* International Society for Technology in Education (Eugene, OR: 1990).
2. G. Bitter and S. Davis, "Measuring the Development of Computer Literacy among Teachers," *AEDS Journal* 18, no. 4 (1985): 243-53.
3. W. Lamon, "Using Computers in Elementary Schools: The 1987 Oregon Assessment," *SIGTE Bulletin,* State Dept. of Education, Salem, OR (ED 323991, 1988): 4.

4. M. Wiske and P. Zodiates, *How Technology Affects Teaching*, NTIS order no. PB88. 202, 22/AS (1988): 6.
5. C. Dwyer, C. Ringstaff, and J. Sandholtz, "*Teacher Beliefs and Practices. Part II: Support for Change. The Evolution of Teachers' Instructional Beliefs and Practices in High-Accesst-to-Technology Classrooms, First to Fourth Year Findings*," ACOT report no. 9 (Apple Classrooms of Tomorrow, Advanced Technology Group, Apple Computer, Inc., 1990): 17.
6. J. Kulik, "Effects of Computer Based Learning on Learners" (paper presented at the National Forum of the College Board Symposium of Computers, Competency, and the Curriculum. Dallas, TX, October 1983).
7. M. Cosden, "Microcomputer Instruction and Perceptions of Effectiveness by Special and Regular Education Elementary School Teachers" *Journal of Special Education* 22, no. 2 (1988): 242-53.
8. H. Becker, *Instructional Uses of School Computers* 1 (Baltimore, MD: The Johns Hopkins University, Center for Social Organization of Schools, 1986).
9. C. Fletcher-Flinn and B. Gravatt, "The Efficacy of Computer Assisted Instruction (CAI): A Meta-analysis," *Journal of Educational Computing Research* 1, no.12 (1995): 219-42.
10. R. Clark, "Evidence for Confounding in Computer Based Instruction Studies: Analyzing the Meta-analysis," *Educational Communication and Technical Journal* 4, no. 4 (1985): 249-62.
11. M. Roblyer, *The Impact of Microcomputer Based Instruction on Teaching and Learning: A Review of Recent Research* (ERIC Clearing House on Information Resources, Syracuse, NY 1988).
12. Ibid.
13. J. Kulik, "Effects of Computer Based Learning on Learners" (paper presented at the National Forum of the College Board Symposium of Computers, Competence, and the Curriculum Dallas, TX, October 1983).
14. J. Kulik, "Computer Based Instruction: What 200 Evaluations Say" (paper presented at the Annual Convention of the Association of Educational Communication and Technology, Atlanta, GA, February 1987).
15. D. Hawley, et. al. "Costs, Effects, and Utility of Microcomputers," *Assisted Instructional Technological Report*, no. 1 (University of Oregon, November 1986).

16. T. Schlechter, "What Do We Really Know about Small Group CAI?" (paper presented at the Annual Conference of The Association for the Development of Computer Based Instructional Systems, St. Louis, MI, ED 342381, November 1991).

17. M. Cosden, "Microcomputer Instruction and Perceptions of Effectiveness by Special and Regular Education Elementary School Teachers" *Journal of Special Education* 22, no. 2 (1988): 242-53.

18. R. Clark, "Evidence for Confounding in Computer Based Instruction Studies: Analyzing the Meta-analysis," *Educational Communication and Technical Journal* 4, no. 4 (1985): 249-62

19. Ibid.

20. Ibid.

21. A. Glenn and C. Carrier, "Perspective on Teacher Technology Training," *Educational Technology* 29, no. 3 (March 1989): 7.

22. E. O'Donnell, "Teacher Perceptions of Their Personal Computer Needs to Integrate Computers into Their Classroom Instruction," (Ed.D diss., University of Southern California, 1991).

23. The Holmes Group, *Tomorrow's Teachers: A Report of the Holmes Group,* East Lansing College of Education, Michigan State University (1986).

Chapter 5

SUSTAINED COMPUTER ASSISTANCE FOR TEACHERS

Many teachers have become aware of the usefulness of computers in education; however, to fully integrate computers into instruction, it is necessary to go beyond the awareness level. The growth in computer awareness among teachers is impressive, as evidenced in the results of research studies that have found that teachers desire training to integrate computers into their classroom instruction. However, training necessarily must go beyond the awareness and hands-on levels to offer teachers the skills necessary to fully integrate computers into their classroom instruction. The number of teachers who require computer training continues to rise. Therefore, there must be an effort to facilitate the acquisition of effective and continuing appropriate professional development for all teachers.

Staff development programs of the past focused on computer literacy, which meant offering the history of computers, keyboarding, and computer programming for teachers. This focus has had direct implications on the type of training that classroom teachers receive and on how computers have been used in instruction. However, this emphasis is not directly applicable to the skills that teachers need to integrate computers into the classroom. Therefore, this approach may have had a negative influence on the large majority of teachers, particularly of the craft culture.

As computers entered more classrooms, it became apparent that the needs of teachers were not being adequately addressed. School districts formed technology committees to study and conduct staff development training. Computer-using teachers were identified to become computer consultants for non-computer-using teachers. Computer coordinators grew from this effort of school districts to utilize computer-using teachers to educate their peers to use computers in the classroom. Researchers recognize some of the problems of utilizing computer coordinators as teacher trainers.[1]

This approach has not been without problems. These efforts were successful for teachers of the technical culture who sought additional computer training. However, teachers of the craft culture did not become enthusiastic enough to seek additional training. Teachers of the technical culture on each campus became valued persons to assist with the computer training of their colleagues.

Need for Professional Instructional Design Technologists

The computer guru, no matter how excellent his or her hands-on computer skills, does not possess the appropriate instructional strategies to assist teachers effectively with integration of computers into the classroom. Teachers require student-centered strategies and computer-centered whole class pedagogical techniques that lead from traditional methods of instruction. Teachers lack the skills and the sustained support necessary to turn away from traditional methods of instruction. Teachers must embrace the pedagogical strategies that lead to the integration of computers into the classroom curriculum. Teachers require guidance and assistance from professionals who are trained in instructional design and technology to embrace the instructional computer strategies necessary for an electronic classroom.

The instructional design technologist and the school library media technology teacher, working collaboratively, are the appropriate persons to offer the instructional computer training and sustained assistance that teachers require to integrate computers into the classroom. Each school district should employ a qualified instructional design technologist permanently on staff at the district level and a school library media technology teacher at each school site to fully integrate computers into the classroom.

At the district level, the responsibilities of the instructional design technologist include the design, development, and the implementation of in-service computer training for classroom teachers. The instructional design technologist is also responsible for the master plan for computer integration and technology resources. Working collaboratively to implement in-service training, the instructional design technologist and the school library media technology teacher can implement a sustained training program that results in the full integration of computers into the classroom.

School Library Media Technology Teacher

The school library media technology teacher is the primary link between traditional methods of instruction and teaching methods required by the merging of technology and print resources. The traditional image of a librarian as only a dispenser of books is no longer a valid image. The library media technology teacher is the professional who links the traditional teacher of the past with the teacher of tomorrow who is comfortable and confident with computers in the classroom. She or he is the campus professional who possesses a knowledge of instructional design, classroom curriculum, teacher-directed instructional strategies, software, hardware, and technology that are encompassed by computer integration into the classroom.

The school library media technology center is an information center that blends the utilization of all resources, both print and non-print, with the classroom and is staffed with a professional media technology teacher who understands both the resources of books and computers as well as the total range of technology on campus. The library media director is the ideal person to assist teachers with the integration of computers into the classroom while serving as a link between district administration, the school principal, and classroom teachers. The library media technology center is the primary link at the school site between the traditional methods of instruction and teaching methods required by the merging of technology and print resources.

The role of the media technology teacher currently encompasses the responsibility of assisting teachers with curriculum and instructional planning in a partnership manner.[2] This partnership encompasses the duties of instructional design and assisting teachers with instructional strategies and pedagogical methods, which result in the integration of computers into the classroom curriculum. Media technology teachers assist and instruct teachers and students in the use of new technology, both hardware and software. The school library, as an information technology center, currently contains computers for teacher and student use. It is staffed with a media technology teacher who assists colleagues with technological skills and the acquisition of knowledge.

Computer Labs and the School Library Media Technology Center

A major reason for the lack of computer integration into the classroom is the lack of access to computers. The proper placement of the computers at each school site is a prime factor in classroom computer use. Computer labs have not proved to be the ideal method to enable teachers to utilize computers in the classroom. The computer lab teacher is trained in hands-on computer skills only and does not possess the instructional design knowledge that is required to integrate computers in the classroom. The duties of the computer lab teacher are concerned primarily with teaching students about computers, not with assisting teachers to integrate computers into classroom instruction. In contrast, the library media technology center is an electronic classroom staffed with a media technology teacher who is a partner with classroom teachers in the process of education. The library media technology center is a model of the classroom of the future that currently offers a combination of electronic services, how to find information, and how to utilize information.

The media technology teacher serves as a liaison between the administration and the classroom teacher. The dissemination of information and resources is a major responsibility of the library media technology teacher. However, it is not the primary responsibility. The most important aspect of the role of the media technology teacher is the collaborative duties of working on a partnership basis with the classroom teacher. In this role, the library technology teacher serves as an instructional partner with the classroom teacher.[3]

In this collaborative paradigm, the media technology teacher and the classroom teacher structure classroom instruction jointly.[4] Together as instructional partners, the objectives for instruction are established.[5] The academic content and structural sequence of the instruction are determined, with specific instructional strategies and student-centered whole class activities prescribed. These will determine how the instructional process and the learning product will be evaluated.

In this collaborative process, the classroom teacher is responsible for student level of skills, academic content, and student assessment. The media technology teacher is responsible for determining the appropriate instructional resources, the information skills to access the resources, the instructional design of the course, and the appropriate technology to utilize. The media technology teacher provides the guidance of how to utilize the resources effectively in a classroom setting. The teacher has an on-site partner to work with on a daily basis as a collaborative guide to classroom instructional practices. Computer integration into the instructional process is facilitated in a successful and cost-effective manner.

Library media technology teachers are in a unique position in the school because they work directly and collaboratively with district-level administrators, the instructional design technologist, school principals, and classroom teachers. The duties of the media technology teacher are varied, but the most important (and the primary responsibility of this teacher) is the collaborative instructional partnership with classroom teachers.

The media technology teacher is the school site professional who is able to work in a sustaining partnership basis with teachers to integrate computers in the classroom. By working on a collaborative basis with the instructional design technologist and the classroom teacher, the media technology teacher becomes the coordinating component for integration of computers in the classroom.

In-Service Training: District and School

School districts that do not have an instructional design technologist should acquire one. At the district level, the instructional design technologist will design, develop, and implement the in-service program while working in collaboration with the library technology teacher. Initially, the instructional design technologist should develop a survey questionnaire to determine the teachers' perceived level of computer skills and the areas in which teachers would like to receive training.

At the school site, the media technology teacher assists in the administration of the survey questionnaire. In addition, the media technology teacher prepares a classroom computer diagram of the school that identifies the location of classroom computers and how teachers are utilizing them in instruction. The classroom computer diagram includes specific documentation of the hardware and software. The information should be forwarded to the district instructional design technologist, who will then synthesize the data to form a complete picture of computer use in the district.

With a complete picture of computer use and computer skills at each school site, the instructional design technologist can determine the in-service computer needs of teachers. These data will give a complete overview of the computer skills and instructional computer knowledge of teachers at each grade-level grouping. In-service should be designed, developed, and implemented with a focus on the specific needs of the teachers within each grade-level grouping. These data should be translated to a personal assistance level for each classroom teacher as the in-service program is implemented.

While working on a partnership basis with classroom teachers, the library media technology teacher becomes familiar with the computer skills of classroom teachers. This information serves as an invaluable aid in targeting the specific needs of each group of teachers. During in-service sessions at each school site the school library media technology teacher assists the instructional design technologist in the presentation of in-service sessions.

As follow-up responsibilities, the school library media technology teacher exercises the role of collaboration with receptive teachers by offering personal assistance. Assistance includes guidance for teachers regarding appropriate software, hardware, and student-centered instructional strategies. The media technology teacher becomes familiar with the subject areas and levels of computer skills at which teachers are working. In this manner, the media technology teacher, in collaboration with the instructional design technologist, is prepared to personalize a computer use plan for classroom teachers.

The collaborative effort continues until the classroom teacher feels confident and comfortable with instructional computer use. The collaborative effort between the media technology teacher, the instructional design technologist, and the classroom teacher is cost-effective because existing personnel are utilized in a successful manner. Also, ongoing personal assistance for teachers will reduce the amount of time and number of in-service sessions required to effect integration of computers into the classroom.

Collaborative Instruction

Collaborative instruction between the library media technology teacher and the receptive classroom teacher occurs on a full partnership basis. Instructional planning includes subject, academic content, and ability level of students. The library media technology teacher also works closely with the classroom teacher on a sustained basis to advise and guide the teacher in the computer implementation process. The in-service follow-up activities by the media technology teacher involve a partnership role to assist the classroom teacher in implementing computer software and instructional packages received at in-service sessions.

The library media technology teacher and the instructional design technologist should conduct an active public relations campaign to publicize the instructional computer services of the library media technology center. In addition, the library media technology teacher should become an instructional partner with all receptive teachers. As colleagues observe the model of services and rewards of classroom computer integration, they will be more likely to integrate computers into their classrooms. Consequently, computer integration is accomplished successfully in a cost-effective and personal manner on a sustained basis.

Research has shown that computer integration happens slowly over time. The plan offered in this book recommends an organized, structured manner of integrating computers into the classroom on a consistent basis, as teachers are receptive. Classroom teachers require sustained assistance beyond initial in-service sessions. The synergy of shared support for classroom teachers will provide the sustaining factor necessary for classroom teachers to gain confidence in their computer abilities and to fully integrate computers into classroom instruction.

Notes

1. A. November, "The Emerging Role of the Computer Coordinator" *Electronic Learning* 4, 4 (1990): 8-9; M. Handler, "Computer Coordinator's Network: Filling a Collegial Void" (paper presented at the Technology and Teacher Education Conference, Greenville, NC, ED 322 112, 11 May 1990): 14; N. Strudler and M. Gall, "Successful Change Agent Strategies for Overcoming Impediments to Microcomputer Implementation in the Classroom" (paper presented at the Annual Meeting of the American Resaerch Association, New Orleans, LA, April 1988): 23
2. *Information Power: Guidelines for School Library Media Programs*, American Association of School Librarians (American Library Association) and Association for Educational Communications and Technology, Washington, D.C.: American Library Association and Association for Educational Communications and Technology, 1988.
3. Ibid.

4. Ibid.
5. N. Dick, "Strategies for Collaboration," *Journal of California Media and Library Educators Association* 17, no. 2 (1994): 21-24.

Chapter 6

A PROCESS OF TIME

Educators are faced with considerable work in bringing teachers to a successful level of instructional computing. In order to move to the next level of training, there must be a complete restructuring of staff development, both preservice and in-service. The task for school districts alone to effectively train large numbers of teachers has proved to be overwhelming. A concerted cooperative effort between school districts and colleges of education is appropriate to offer teachers the type of computer education and training that is necessary for the future of widespread computer integration into the classroom. A systematic well organized approach, from preservice through in-service computer education training, is vital to the success of instructional computer integration.

Since the advent of computers in education, colleges of education and school districts have been working in isolation from each other to meet the computer needs of teachers. Past efforts have resulted in duplication of effort and funds expended without cost-effective results. Each school district and college of education has purchased new equipment and expended large amounts of time and funds to bring teachers to an awareness and hands-on level of instructional computing.

Preservice and In-Service Computer Training

For colleges of education, the need for computer training of teachers has led to the creation of new programs and the revision of existing programs. Colleges of education had to decide where in the preservice curriculum to place computer training, and how much and what kind of training to offer teachers.[1] As part of the program to train teachers for instructional computing, colleges of education have offered basic computer classes for teachers and graduate student programs to prepare computer specialists.[2] Colleges of education have sometimes offered assistance to school districts with the in-service training of their staff; however, this has not been the norm. For the most part, school districts and colleges of education work in isolation from each other. For school districts, this has meant the development of in-service staff training programs that are costly and time consuming. The result is that teachers receive only the most basic of computer skills while some teachers receive no computer training at all.

Both school districts and colleges of education have been faced with critical decisions of what type of computer training to offer teachers.[3] The result has been an inconsistent training of teachers who receive only basic computer skills acquisition and no understanding of classroom computer strategies or pedagogical techniques to utilize with computers in the classroom. Some colleges of education have responded with minimal training, while other institutions have responded with exemplary training for teachers. Most school districts have offered basic computer skills training for teachers; however, many have offered no training for teachers. There are no standards or guidelines for either an institution, school district, or college to follow when framing computer training for teachers. The result has been the inadequate training of teachers, who acquire only basic computer skills.

These first attempts at computer training of teachers have been a necessary learning experience for institutions and have proved to be the first stage in the task of training teachers to integrate computers into classrooms. They have shown that hands-on and awareness training are only a first and necessary step in the training of teachers to use computers effectively in classrooms. These early experiences also have shown that, for the widespread integration of computers in the classroom, the training of teachers must include the instructional skills, the classroom dynamics, and the student-centered strategies that are necessary for the full and widespread integration of computers into the classroom.

Cooperative Effort Needed

The cooperative framing of guidelines between school districts and colleges of education for teacher computer training will allow each to offer the specific training that teachers need. A new paradigm of cooperation is needed between colleges of education and school districts that will prevent duplication of effort, be cost-effective, and offer teachers a higher quality of training.

To integrate computers into instruction, classroom teachers need a basic understanding of teacher-directed and student-centered classroom strategies that lead from traditional methods of instruction to computer-centered instruction. An ongoing period of time is required to gain the knowledge and computer skills necessary to integrate computers into the classroom. The O'Donnell study covered a period of approximately six years. After this period of time, the teachers of the school district were still at the awareness level of classroom computer integration.[4] This indicates that it takes more than six years to accomplish effective computer training of teachers with the current methods of preservice and in-service training. This length of time also indicates a complete review of current methods of training teachers for classroom computer use.

Teacher preservice and in-service must be based exclusively upon teacher needs, from the placement of computers to the instructional strategies that teachers require to integrate computers into the classroom curriculum. The length of time needed for the training of teachers indicates that a cooperative effort between school districts and colleges of education is necessary. Neither should work in isolation. Complete cooperation for the successful computer training of teachers is called for. Each cooperating institution should establish a professional position that is responsible for the program of cooperation. This author recommends that this professional position be filled with an instructional design technologist.

Before undertaking any preservice or in-service program, the instructional design technologist at each institution should identify teachers' needs and communicate these to the cooperating institution. This information serves to determine not only what teacher in-service needs are, but also what preservice computer skills and pedagogical training should be taught. A clear identification of teacher-perceived needs is necessary to establish the parameters of both preservice and in-service education.

No Consensus Concerning Competencies

Currently, there is no consensus concerning the competencies that teachers need to integrate computers into classrooms.[5] This book sets forth the theory that the teacher is the key to instructional computing. Without initially considering teacher needs in all staff development efforts, there will be little or no progress. Without offering teacher-directed computer methods and instructional strategies one cannot expect much progress in instructional computing.

The majority of teachers are still somewhat reluctant to incorporate computers into their instruction. Therefore, staff development training programs must be designed and developed specifically with classroom teachers as the focus. The classroom teacher is the key to successful integration of computers in the classroom. It is of primary importance to identify the specific instructional computer needs of teachers before undertaking a staff development program.

Teachers Are the Key

Designing staff development programs is complicated by the fact that teachers demonstrate varying instructional computing needs at different grade levels and at varying levels of personal computing skills. In addition, at each grade-level grouping, teachers list a different computer skill for which they desire additional computer training. This factor has not been addressed in past staff development computer training programs. It is imperative that, before a district undertakes staff development for the integration of computers into the curriculum, teachers of the district are surveyed to identify their specific instructional computing needs. All in-service sessions should be designed specifically to focus upon identified teacher needs.

As stated in chapter 5, it is strongly suggested that a degreed instructional design technologist be employed at the district level on a full-time permanent basis to design and develop in-service instructional computer programs which focus on teacher needs and to coordinate computer in-service with a cooperating college of education. By working closely with library media technology teachers and classroom teachers, the instructional design technologist becomes knowledgeable about the computer skills of the teachers and is able to develop in-service programs designed specifically for teacher needs at each grade-level grouping.

To integrate computers into the classroom, all teachers need an understanding of how the computer works, and of keyboarding skills. However, of equal importance is the acquisition of student-centered classroom strategies and the knowledge of how to merge instructional computing with the daily classroom curriculum. The use of classroom computers is often restricted to lecture-centered instructional techniques that can be easily incorporated into traditional instruction. The majority of teachers do not feel confident in utilizing computers in a manner that requires a change in traditional methods of instruction.

Modes of Computer Integration

To enable classroom teachers to make effective changes in classroom dynamics, sustained computer support is necessary. The acquisition of an instructional design technologist permanently on staff enhances the integration of computers into the classroom by providing the sustained assistance that enables teachers to go beyond drill and practice and the use of computer games. These activities are appropriate in some instructional settings and serve as a beginning for classroom computer use; however, this is not computer integration. Computer training of classroom teachers must move beyond the initial stage of classroom computer utilization through the total process that integrates computers into the classroom curriculum.

Apple Computer, Inc., has found that this process encompasses teachers' beliefs about computers in the classroom. These beliefs include but are not limited to the teacher's beliefs concerning computers and a personal level of mastery of computers.[6] O'Donnell found that this process also includes teachers' perceptions of which instructional strategy to employ with instructional software and the appropriate pedagogical methods to utilize with computers in instruction.[7] In a meta-analysis of computer studies some researchers found questions concerning the efficacy of computers in instruction.[8]

There are various processes involved in the instructional use of computers that help to frame teachers' belief system concerning computers. These processes are part of an interlocking network between teachers, students, and computer instruction that are evident at all levels of computer integration. Computers are never used in the classroom in an isolated manner. They interact with classroom dynamics. The key to instructional computer use is altering teachers beliefs and practices slowly in such a manner that they feel comfortable with computers at each stage of progress.

Teachers must be guided comfortably through the process of integrating computers into the classroom. The process of replacing traditional teaching methods with instructional methods that embrace computers involves a multiplicity of factors and an ongoing process of growth. This process of growth is facilitated by offering teachers an interlocking continuum of computer skills acquired over time in a manner that allows for the internal processing of a changing belief system and the acquisition of a structured sequence of instructional computing skills. The process of time is necessary to compensate for the replacement of changing pedagogical practices while traditional teaching practices are being replaced with newer techniques.

Change in Belief System

The integration of computers into the classroom presents a personal challenge to classroom teachers. The degree of integration achieved and the time required for teachers to learn how to fully utilize computers in the classroom is dependent upon the perceived beliefs of the teacher concerning computers and their use in instruction. Integration is a necessarily slow process. Beliefs are not changed quickly. However, the perceived beliefs of the teacher will guide and drive the teacher toward the goal of computer integration. Beliefs are framed slowly and are dependent upon education, knowledge, and personal experience of self and others.

Teachers first use computers to reinforce traditional instruction, then slowly begin to adapt their instruction to utilize computers in more sophisticated ways as their beliefs about and skills with computers change.[9] Eventually, teachers begin to explore the potential of instructional computing. As belief systems change, a realization of the possibilities of computers in the classroom is discovered.[10] An appreciation of teacher-directed learning techniques and student-centered computer strategies leads to a desire to acquire those skills. Teachers then find that traditional methods of teaching do not meet their enhanced beliefs concerning the instructional use of computers.

This is the primary reason why it has been difficult for school districts to achieve full computer integration into the classroom. The process of changing perceived beliefs cannot be hurried.[11] Teachers must be trained away from traditional methods of classroom instruction over a period of time.[12]

Many colleges of education train teachers in traditional methods of instruction. In addition, the majority of school administrators and principals expect teachers to utilize traditional methods of instruction. However, in a brief, inadequate training period, teachers are expected to embrace new skills, new knowledge, and new beliefs concerning computers in the classroom. This has not happened in the past and will not happen in the future.

Notes

1. D. Gooler, "Preparing Teachers to Use Technologies: Can Universities Meet the Challenge?" *Educational Technology* 29, no. 3, (March 1989): 18; A. Glenn and C. Carrier, "A Perspective on Teacher Technology Training" *Educational Technology* 29 no. 3, (March 1989): 18.
2. Gooler, "Preparing Teachers."
3. Ibid.
4. E. O'Donnell, "Teacher Perceptions Concerning Their Personal Computer Needs to Integrate Computers into Their Classroom Instruction" (Ed. D. diss. University of Southern California,1991): 2-3.
5. J. Bruwelheide, "Teacher Competencies for Microcomputer Use in the Classroom: A Literature Review" *Educational Technology* 22, no. 10 (1982): 29-30.
6. D. Dwyer, C. Ringstaff, and J. Sandholtz, *Teacher Beliefs and Practices. Part I: Patterns of Change. The Evolution of Teachers' Instructional Beliefs and Practices in High-Access-to-Technology Classrooms, First-Fourth Year Findings* ACOT report no. 8 (Apple Classrooms of Tomorrow, Advanced Technology Group, Apple Computer, Inc., 1990).
7. E. O'Donnell, "Teacher Perceptions," 88-89.
8 C. Kulik and J. Kulik, "Effectiveness of Computer-Based Instruction: An Updated Analysis," *Computers in Human Behavior* 7, no. 7 (1991): 75-94; C. Fletcher-Flinn and B. Gravatt "The Efficacy of Computer Assisted Instruction (CAI): A Meta-analysis," *Journal of Educational Computing Research* 12, no. 3, (1995): 210-41.
9. D. Dwyer, C. Ringstaff, and J. Sandholtz, *Teacher Beliefs and Practices.*
10. Ibid.
11. Ibid.
12. Ibid.

Chapter 7

COOPERATIVE PARADIGM

Broad, general guidelines for staff development may be utilized across districts or for colleges of education when developing programs of staff development training for computer preservice and in-service. However, programs of training must answer the varying needs of the teachers for which they are intended. This chapter offers an organizational framework in which colleges and school districts can insert their unique data when developing and designing staff development programs for the integration of computers into the classroom.

The cooperative framing of guidelines for the computer education of teachers is required to achieve the slow but necessary change in belief systems and teaching practices that is required for computer integration. It has proved to be impossible for either the school district or the college alone to fully train teachers to assume the responsibility of integrating computers into instruction. A paradigm of full partnership between colleges of education and school districts will produce the desired goal of computer integration on a widespread basis in American schools.

Professional staff trained specifically for computer integration in the classroom must assume the duties of training teachers on a long-term and cooperative basis. Too often professors who are not computer literate and a school district staff that is trained in hands-on skills only are responsible for the computer training of teachers. Only trainers who possess a knowledge of successful computer strategies in a classroom setting should be responsible for training teachers in the instructional use of computers.

Teacher needs for computer integration in the whole class setting must be met if widespread use of computers in the classroom is to be realized. Professors who are computer knowledgeable at the college level and the instructional design technologist at the school district level must frame computer guidelines and train teachers jointly. Each should become a welcome visitor to the classroom of the cooperating institution.

Identification of Instructional Computer Needs

Researchers must study the instructional use of computers in the classroom setting where the critical factors leading to and involved in the full integration of computers can be studied in all their complexity. Isolation of these factors from the classroom for study cannot be done in a reliable manner because they are interlocking and interdependent. This multiplicity of instructional factors shapes the classroom teacher's belief system concerning computer integration. The classroom teacher cannot be separated from the study of computer integration or from the instructional setting in which the computer is to be utilized. Therefore, a strong cooperative effort between school districts and colleges of education is called for in the design, development, and implementation of computer training programs for the classroom teacher. As part of this effort, teachers must become comfortable with researchers in the classroom. This manner of cooperation will enable reliable, cost-effective, and long-range master plans to be developed that will answer teacher needs for full and facile integration of computers into instruction. The full cooperation of both institutions will serve to transform teacher beliefs slowly as their training progresses.

Focused Master Plan

The most important aspect of planning for the integration of computers into the classroom is the overall master plan which serves as a beacon for all future planning. A focused master plan, written in specific, easy-to-understand terms and widely distributed to all staff members, is essential. Many school districts have formulated master plans written in rhetorical terms so general that they do not offer the direction that the district requires to merge computers into the curriculum. In a similar manner, comprehensive master technology plans that address a full range of technology will not lead to the integration of computers into the classroom. Master plans for computer integration must be directed in a focused manner toward computers in the classroom. A tightly written, specifically focused master plan that deals only with computers in the classroom is necessary for successful staff development. When a plan for computer integration in the classroom is included in the overall technology plan, computers in the classroom are not the focus and computer integration tends to become lost within the overall plan for technology. An effective computer integration plan must focus on teacher needs and the strategic instructional activities that are necessary to implement computers into whole class instruction.

Visions of Computer Integration

Professional rhetoric cloaked in general terms does not offer the guidance necessary to form a blueprint of computer integration. Rather, a focus on specific implementation activities stated in easy-to-understand terms is necessary and effective. Highly organized and specifically focused master plans are a necessary part of the strategic planning that is required to implement computers into instruction.

Initially, a vision of computer integration may be dramatic and exciting, but it is not sufficient to serve as a working plan. A vision is somewhat ethereal and somewhat transparent and may even provide the illusion of focused activity. Visions are the thoughts that dreams are made of; however, they quickly fade when initial enthusiasm wanes. A vision must be translated into tangible form, which serves as a firm foundation for future action. Visions must be described in concrete terms, then broken into units that form the components of strategic planning, which then can be stated in goal form and focused into action.

A vision can be broken into easily managed working parts that combine to comprise a whole. By carefully dissecting the vision into component parts, a master plan that is tightly structured can be developed. Too often, school districts try to grasp the total ethereal vision in an impulsive manner that does not encompass the verity of the multiplicity of factors involved. By working with the component parts, visions become reality through the formulation of easily achieved goals.

A vision consists of three major components that can be dissected into easily managed parts. The major components of a vision are organizing, planning, and implementing. In this conceptualization, organizing concerns the cooperation between the college of education and the school district. Planning deals with the formulation of a master plan and strategic planning. Implementation concerns the activities that are required to achieve full computer integration into classroom instruction.

The acquisition of an instructional design technologist at the district level and a school library media technology teacher at each school site will greatly facilitate the process of implementation in a cost-effective manner. Organization, strategic planning, and a professional staff capable of training and sustaining classroom teachers as they introduce computers into the classroom, are necessary to bring the vision to fruition.

Organizing Component

The overall responsibility for organizing and strategic planning lies with the instructional design technologist. A major responsibility is the organization of the cooperative effort with the college of education. Initially, the cooperating college of education is identified and contacted. Next, a computer integration committee is formed at the district level. This committee should include classroom teachers who assist with initial decisions and organizing efforts.

Telephone or electronic contact should be made with the college of education located closest to the school district. Liaison and articulation efforts can then begin between the cooperating institution and the school district. The times and dates for meetings should be jointly scheduled on a regular basis.

The responsibility of each institution is defined during the initially scheduled meetings. The college of education is responsible for preservice education, and the school district is responsible for in-service. Cooperation should continue throughout the duration of the training program. Arrangements should be made for preservice teachers to enter the classrooms of the school district to work as teacher assistants for the duration of the preservice training period.

Cooperative arrangements should be made for the college of education to assist the school district with in-service training of practicing teachers. The cooperative responsibilities of each training program should be established early in the planning and organizing process. The computer skills and knowledge offered should progress from hands-on through a complete understanding of computers in the classroom. Each institution should offer reinforcing skills and classroom strategies but not duplicate efforts. The specific areas of training that each institution is responsible for should be clearly established and defined so that efforts are not duplicated.

Planning Component

Preservice and in-service training for computer integration into the classroom should not be organized and planned in isolation. School districts and colleges of education must plan training in a joint cooperative effort to offer teachers the computer instructional skills that they require to utilize computers in the classroom. Both preservice and in-service must be comprehensively and systematically planned. The cooperative link between the K-12 level and colleges of education must be strengthened. Teachers must be trained in an organized manner that offers a structured sequence of computer skills that progresses to a level of student-centered and teacher-directed classroom techniques that enable teachers to integrate computers into the classroom. Hands-on skills are necessary; however, training must not stop there. When teachers do not acquire the instructional skills required for computer integration in a classroom setting, computer integration rests on a fragile foundation.

The computer training of teachers is currently fragmented, with no visible structure between preservice and in-service. Efforts are duplicated and, with few exceptions, training does not progress beyond hands-on computer skills in either preservice or in-service. The cooperative planning of preservice and in-service training programs offers teachers a comprehensive understanding of the role of computers in the classroom, while allowing teachers to acquire the student-centered instructional strategies that will fulfill their needs for computer integration in the classroom.

As with in-service, there is little attempt in preservice to deliver computer instruction as a fully integrated component of instruction. Computer training is usually still offered as a separate course, isolated from the teacher education curriculum. Usually, entry-level teachers have received hands-on training only and have never experienced an environment where computers have been merged with the curriculum. In this setting, teachers cannot develop a broad understanding of the instructional role of the computer. The hands-on approach to teacher training does not provide a broad range of computer skills or an understanding of how to manage instruction in the whole class setting utilizing computers.

Implementation Component

Teachers must have the necessary skills to manage a whole class setting with computers where several different instructional activities may be taking place simultaneously. These enabling factors for computer integration must be addressed at both the preservice and the in-service levels in a structured, cooperative, and well-planned manner. Future teachers must acquire a realistic view of the role of a practicing teacher while acquiring practical experience. In addition, cooperative arrangements with a conveniently located college of education result in better trained teachers and are cost-effective for each institution.

The cooperating college of education and the school district should be aligned in a mutual agreement of autonomy unified by the common goal of preparing teachers for computer integration in the classroom. The college of education should provide education and leadership, with the district providing experience for prospective teachers. The cooperative link between the school district and college should lead to an identification of the instructional computer needs of teachers through reliable research conducted in the classroom of successful computer-using teachers. After identification of teacher instructional computer needs, the school district and the college of education should unite in the planning, implementation, and evaluation of a unified staff development program.

Since the multiplicity of factors affecting classroom use of computers and the specific competencies which teachers require for integration of computers in instruction have not been identified, an identification of teacher computer needs and a paradigm of cooperation between school districts and colleges of education is imperative for the future training of classroom teachers. Cooperative efforts between school districts and colleges of education, formed with the goal of producing better trained classroom teachers, will lead to an identification of the factors that enable computer use as an instructional tool and the full integration of computers into the classroom.

Paradigm of Cooperation

In this paradigm of cooperation, school districts communicate clearly the computer training that teachers require to fully integrate computers into a classroom setting. In order to strengthen rather than to duplicate efforts, the responsibility for the training of preservice and in-service teachers should be by mutual agreement. Cooperative training activities include a program of continuing education for in-service teachers and training of preservice teachers in the classrooms of the school district. The responsibility for training preservice and in-service teachers is by mutual agreement and with full cooperation of the cooperating institution.

The identification and dissemination of knowledge regarding classroom computer training falls within the domain of both institutions. To facilitate and assist in the identification of specific student-centered strategies to integrate computers into instruction, research professors should have full access to classrooms. Staff development efforts of the cooperating institutions should be merged into a unified whole in order to bring continuity and structure to preservice and in-service computer training.

Cooperative Planning

Initial planning should be done on a cooperative basis to establish the responsibilities and the paradigm of training for each institution. Strategic planning for efforts within the unique parameters of each institution should be done on an institutional basis. At the school district, planning should include all classroom teachers who wish to participate. Teachers' workloads should not be increased because of a wish to serve on computer planning committees. Thus, teachers serving on planning committees should receive release time and a shortened schedule. Department chairs and the school library media technology teacher should also be included in all planning sessions.

Strategic planning is the foundation of successful in-service. Before time or funds are expended, a comprehensive plan for computer implementation should be developed. The cooperative plan in this book encompasses a long-range and ongoing perspective of computer integration that defines specific educational goals of implementation. Cooperative strategic planning requires an examination of the opportunities of preservice instructional computer training and how the district can coordinate in-service with preservice training of the cooperating college. A firm commitment by the district to fund and to continue in-service training on a sustained basis is necessary.

Classroom Teacher as Pivotal to Successful Computer Training

A preferred and cost-effective plan is characterized by strategic planning with the cooperating college of education which offers preservice training for teachers. The district in-service plan should enhance and build on the preservice program for teachers. Cooperative planning prevents duplication of effort and offers teachers ongoing training that answers their needs for experience in a classroom setting. Currently, preservice does not include practical knowledge of classroom procedures and dynamics. Preservice teachers should experience instructional computer training in a whole class setting with a master teacher who is experienced with student centered- strategies that are necessary for the integration of computers into the classroom.

Highly focused strategic planning that establishes overall direction while offering specific implementation strategies will ensure an effective in-service program. Strategic planning defines direction while offering the framework of specific activities for implementation. The overall plan must be focused while retaining the flexibility to address the continuing needs of teachers.

Strategic implementation of computer integration in the classroom must recognize that the classroom teacher is pivotal to the implementation process. This process cannot happen on a widespread basis without changing the belief system of the classroom teacher, beginning with preservice. Teachers must believe that computers are an instructional asset, that the integration process will be easy to accomplish, and that computers will be conveniently available. After the belief system has changed and full acceptance of computers is accomplished, to deny teachers easy access to computers will result in continued nonsupport of computer integration in the classroom.

Implementation of Computers in the Classroom

There are enabling factors that must be addressed at both district and college levels to make computer use more accessible for teachers. One of these factors is the location of computers. Many professors and teachers do not use computers because of the difficulty of obtaining access to a computer. The majority of computers are found in computer labs where access is difficult for professors and classroom teachers.

Principals and college administrators should assess the goals of computer placement. If the goal is student access to computers, then a computer lab setting, where students can become computer literate, is appropriate. However, if the goal is for professors and teachers to integrate computers into classroom instruction, then computers should be placed in the classrooms. It has proven difficult for professors and teachers to gain access to a computer lab where students utilize the computers for hands-on practice or where computer literacy classes are taught. In addition, professors and classroom teachers do not wish to be placed in a learning situation with students whom they may have in class, and computer literacy teachers are not prepared to teach professors or teachers the student-centered instructional strategies that are required for the integration of computers into the classroom.

Computer labs are staffed with a hands-on person, often on a part-time basis, or a computer teacher whose major task is to teach computer literacy to students. When a professor or teacher wishes to use the computers, the class must be moved to the lab. Valuable teaching time is lost, the teacher's possible lack of computer skill is exposed, and students lose their focus on the lesson. In addition, a computer lab is not the proper setting to teach subject content utilizing computers. These educational problems quickly stifle a professor or a teacher's enthusiasm.

Computer Labs Are for Students

Computer labs at both colleges and schools are necessary for the purpose for which they are best suited: to teach computer literacy to students. If computer labs are to be utilized for a dual purpose, the lab should be placed in the college library or the school library media technology center. In such a center a self-contained classroom setting is available where the library media technology teacher is able to provide the sustained assistance for professors or classroom teachers that may be required to integrate computers into the curriculum.

It is understandable that computer labs for student use must be acquired. However, if funding is not available for the acquisition of computers for every teacher's classroom, then computers should be placed in the library media technology center, which is staffed with a competent computer and instructional professional. The library media technology center may be used as a lab or classroom by any teacher who wishes to have access. When utilizing the library media center as a computer lab, it should be staffed by a computer lab teacher, as well as a library media technology teacher.

Computer integration for the classroom teacher has often been like offering candy to babies and removing it when they reach for it. In the past, professors and teachers have changed their belief system, gone through computer training, and then been denied a computer in the classroom or convenient access to computers. Teachers and professors must be given access to computers in a self-contained classroom setting. Districts should allot funding for computers as initial planning begins. An intense level of commitment and funds must be fully supported before embarking upon a computer training effort. Too often, districts and colleges have not sufficiently funded or supported teachers and professors in their efforts to achieve computer integration.

A Framework for Cooperative Planning

The following guidelines are general enough to allow colleges and school districts to insert their individual educational characteristics into the framework. The major components of planning are the same for each district or college; however, the specific plans and the implementation process will vary. These guidelines are purposefully flexible to ensure individual ownership by each school. These frameworks allow school districts or colleges a continued process of implementation that ensures full integration of computers into the classroom. An implementation plan that is nonstatic, but alive, and flexible enough to encompass the unique situations of each institution should result from the use of these guidelines.

The instructional design technologist coordinates the initial effort by forming a committee to guide the cooperative efforts of the school district, by establishing initial telephone or electronic contact with the nearest college of education, and by serving as a liaison between the two institutions.

The instructional design technologist will also schedule regular meetings at each campus with the sprecific persons who are responsible for preservice and in-service training of teachers and will participate in the cooperative planning of these programs of computer education for teachers at both institutions.

The college of education will offer teacher education classes which fully integrate computers into the instruction to serve as a model for preservice teachers. The cooperating college should offer continuing education classes in computer integration at convenient times for practicing teachers. The college should also incorporate extensive instructional computer education that emphasizes whole class teacher-directed and student-centered strategies as part of all preservice training courses for prospective teachers, and should require classroom instructional computer experience for all preservice teachers. Courses should be required for preservice teachers which emphasize the use of computers as an instructional tool.

Professors and researchers should have access to the classrooms of the cooperating district on an ongoing basis so that they become thoroughly familiar with classroom dynamics and instructional computing needs. Professors and researchers should also exert an interdisciplinary effort to identify the factors contributing to the most effective teacher-directed and student-centered teaching strategies.

As partners in education the cooperating institutions should assess the perceived instructional computer needs of the teachers, synthesize the information into the computer training program, and frame programs of preservice and in-service computer training based specifically on the identified needs of the teachers.

Chapter 8

THE MISSING KEY

There is a widespread belief in education that hands-on skills taught in isolation from classroom practices will lead the integration of computers into the instructional process. This has not happened, and it will not happen. The process of staff development must combine instructional design and student and teacher instructional strategies with computer skills before computers are to be integrated into instruction on a widespread basis.

There is a specific interaction between knowledge and skill. The learning of skills and development of cognitive knowledge interact and cannot be separated. Computer instruction should be directed toward acquisition of instructional knowledge and computer skills combined as a wholistic process appropriate for a whole class setting. Development of knowledge and skills in isolation from each other is meaningless to teachers.

Neither cognitive knowledge nor hands-on skills alone will allow teachers to acquire an interactive classroom stance. Preservice and in-service training must synchronize and merge cognitive knowledge with hands-on skills to allow for full classroom integration of computers. The process of knowledge and skills acquisition is a gradual process that requires an integrated training process. The learning of new knowledge needs to be combined with the training of hands-on skills to utilize this knowledge. The acquisition of skills and knowledge cannot be separated.

Acquisition of Instructional Strategies

The cognitive instructional knowledge involved with the integration of computers has been almost totally ignored in teacher in-service. The research of O'Donnell has shown that teachers not only need but also wish to receive the cognitive instructional knowledge necessary to work with students and to design and develop instruction that will effectively integrate computers into the curriculum.[1]

Administrators have been disappointed in their expectation that teachers would successfully and readily integrate computers into instruction on a widespread basis by offering only hands-on computer skills in-service computer training programs. Teachers must have hands-on computer skills, but they must also acquire the ability to identify and transform traditional instruction to computer-enhanced instruction. This process requires acquisition of cognitive knowledge that teachers are not being offered in current instructional computer preservice and in-service programs. To move to the widespread integration of computers into classroom instruction, there must be a blending of hands-on computer skills with the knowledge of instructional techniques that lead from traditional instruction to a wholistic classroom that merges computers with the instructional process. Teachers must possess the capacity to link knowledge of instructional strategies and computer hands-on skills. Preservice and in-service must merge these dual skills into a continuity of instructional computer acquisition, which leads directly to the integration of computers into the curriculum.

Cognitive Schematic for Computer Integration

Teachers must possess a cognitive schematic for integrating computers into the classroom curriculum. Constructivist learning theory suggests that learning devoid of context may be shallow and incomplete.[2] Information is best learned in context with experiences of knowledge and skill combined and merged into a total wholistic process. Teaching only hands-on skills strips the training of cognitive knowledge and does not allow teachers to acquire the interactive teaching strategies they must possess to confidently and successfully integrate computers into the classroom.

Providing teachers with a simulated classroom experience with computers through contextual training offers them a wholistic class-room experience. This experience offers them a meaningful situation in which to develop required instructional classroom strategies and computer skills simultaneously. In this manner, knowledge and skills are embedded in an experience that is easily transferred to an actual classroom environment. It is cognitive knowledge, transferred to a meaningful situation, which changes the behavior of the teacher.[3]

Successful transfer of skills depends upon cognitive knowledge merged with hands-on skills in a context of theory and practice that is easily transferred to a classroom environment. Preservice and in-service is more than the acquisition of a series of hands-on skills. It is a complex process that is based upon the acquisition of cognitive knowledge and skills acquisition which are readily transferred to the classroom. Teachers must learn to successfully modify and adapt traditional instruction to a wholistic classroom situation that encompasses the use of computers. Full integration of computers into the classroom requires teacher confidence and transfer of knowledge from preservice and in-service training sessions to the classroom.

The cognitive knowledge for successful classroom computer integration must be explicitly included in all in-service sessions. In-service computer training programs have largely been unsuccessful because of a failure to contribute to teacher performance in the classroom. The primary reason for the failure of computer in-service programs to impact classroom practice has been the tendency to concentrate on hands-on skills while ignoring teacher-directed instructional strategies. Teacher-driven instructional strategies are the key to the integration of computers in the classroom. A recognition of the importance of a whole class environment links training to performance in a meaningful manner.

Notes

1. E. O'Donnell, "Teacher Perceptions Concerning Their Personal Computer Needs to Integrate Computers into Their Classroom Instruction" (Ed.D. diss. University of Southern California, 1991).
2. D. Jonassen, "Thinking Technology: Context Is Everything." *Educational Technology* 31, no. 6, (1991): 35.
3. B. Showers, B. Joyce, and B. Bennett "Synthesis of Research on Staff Development: A Framework for Future Study and a State-of-the-Art Analysis," *Educational Leadership, Journal of the Association for Supervision and Curriculum Development* 45, no. 3 (1987): 77-87.

Chapter 9

A SURVEY QUESTIONNAIRE

The experiences of the following school district will serve as an illustration of the sincere efforts of a school district to in-service classroom teachers in the absence of guidelines for the integration of computers into the classroom. Unlike this district, however, the majority of school districts do not have any follow-up to the initial in-service. Also, most school districts are not as consistent and persistent in their efforts to meet teacher needs.

The district surveyed 728 classroom teachers in the school district concerning their classroom computer needs. The responses identified specific proficiencies and strategies that classroom teachers believe they need to utilize computers in the classroom. The results of the survey indicate that there is a need to reexamine the goals of staff development programs being offered by school districts. To achieve full integration of computers into the classroom, the instructional computer needs of teachers must be met. School districts must focus on the classroom instructional computer needs of their teachers when they are framing staff development programs. A focus on teacher needs will enable school districts to design and develop in-service programs that specifically address the identified instructional computer needs that teachers require to fully integrate computers into the classroom. The majority of staff development programs do not consider the perceived needs of the teachers but have approached staff development in a very general manner. This survey is the first study that has considered the perceived needs of a large number of classroom teachers.

In Spring 1991, the District Technology Committee, consisting of a school-site coordinator, a secondary school library media director (O'Donnell), four resource teachers, four school principals, a district specialist, and the district librarian, conducted a computer survey of the teachers in district K-12 classrooms as part of the district's technology master plan. The purpose of the master plan was to establish a direction for infusing technology into the instructional program. Because of a lack of funds, computers had not been placed in classrooms but rather at varying locations in the district depending upon the school site. Students had access to computers in mathematics classrooms, computer labs, library media centers, and on a computer cart that could be moved to various locations at the school site.

In 1984, the committee developed a technology needs assessment based upon a random sampling of 229 administrators and teachers. Using the information gathered in the 1984 survey, a master plan for instructional technology was developed. Based upon the initial master plan and needs assessment of 1984, a series of staff development in-service training sessions were developed. The initial goal of this staff development training program was to bring teachers to an awareness level in the instructional uses of educational technology.

Design of the Teacher Survey and Questionnaire

During the school year 1986-87, the initial phase of in-service training sessions, to bring teachers to an awareness level of computers, was completed. At the conclusion of the in-service training in 1987, the District Technology Committee agreed that it would be beneficial to conduct another survey to assess teacher computer needs before conducting any further in-service training. In 1988, the District Technology Committee approved a survey to assess teacher perceived computer needs on which to base future computer in-service. In 1988-89, another survey was administered by the District Technology Committee to assess the computer awareness of the K-12 classroom teachers.

A questionnaire was developed by O'Donnell to gather information on the skills and computer use of the 728 classroom teachers of the district. The research was conducted in three primary stages. During the first stage, the questionnaire was prepared for approval by the District Technology Committee. Second, the survey was revised four times before the final draft received committee approval. This occurred over approximately two years. Third, the school principals were notified in a special administrative meeting that the survey was to be given to teachers and collected during a regularly scheduled faculty meeting. The principals were given instructions to observe any problem that the teachers might have in interpreting the questions on the survey.

The content of the 1988-89 survey was designed to complement the information gathered in the 1986-87 survey. The district committee felt that it was important, before designing future in-service training, to assess whether teachers had reached an awareness level of instructional computing and in which areas they would like to receive further training.

The sample survey included all classroom teachers in the district, K-12, including special education, English as a second language, and district resource teachers, for a total of 855 teachers. The survey questionnaires were distributed to principals to be given at a regularly scheduled faculty meeting at their respective schools on the same day of the week and the same week of the month throughout the district.

Teachers were given the questionnaire and a Scantron sheet on which to mark their responses. Teachers were instructed to fill out the questionnaire and return it before they left the room. Authorized persons were stationed at the exits to collect the survey as the teachers left. The forms were then returned to the district office during the week. Out of the 855 surveys distributed, 718 completed surveys were returned.

The district office forwarded the survey sheets and the Scantron sheets to the district librarian, who was the chair of the District Technology Committee. A preliminary tabulation was then made to ascertain whether any of the surveys and answer sheets had not been returned. Each principal from the school sites with missing surveys was then contacted and asked to collect the missing surveys and answer sheets and return them to the district librarian. All of the schools with missing surveys responded. However, a 100-percent return rate was not achieved. A final tabulation was made. The final return was 728 surveys, for a return rate of 85 percent.

Instrumentation of the Survey

The questionnaire was designed specifically for the needs of the classroom teachers of the district who had previously received the first phase of computer in-service training in 1986. The questionnaire (see Appendix A) consists of 62 yes-no questions and 4 multiple-choice questions, all closed choice. The survey format was designed for ease of response so that teachers could answer the questions rapidly. In addition, the design was intended to elicit answers that would not require much introspection and could be easily tabulated.

This survey was intended to assess a closed population: the classroom teachers of the district. No formal reliability or validity measures were employed. However, it was recognized that measures of validity are important to ensure that the instrument is appropriate for what it intends to measure. One type of validity is content validity. The District Technology Committee believed this survey has a high level of content validity since the questions were worded specifically for ease of understanding by classroom teachers and the questions clearly assess computer use. The questionnaire was framed around clearly stated objectives, and each item on the questionnaire was directly associated with the specific area in which the committee wished to acquire information concerning the computer usage skills. Four two-hour committee meetings were spent on the wording of the questions to ensure appropriateness and clarity.

Additional evidence of content validity was found in the administration of the survey. As reported by principals, there were no problems associated with understanding any questions on the survey. Moreover, survey responses were anonymous so there was no reason to believe that the teachers were not completely honest in answering the questions on the survey. The survey included three general areas: general information, self-perceived computer skills, and computer use.

The survey was designed specifically to determine the computer requirements that teachers believed would enable them to fulfill their technological role in the learning process. The survey also assessed the instructional use of computers at specific levels of instruction K-12, academic subject areas, and teaching areas such as English as a second language, special education or resource teacher. Resource teachers were included in the survey because they were also classroom teachers. The survey was particularly designed to determine the extent of technological applications being used in classroom instruction and the assessment of projected teacher participation in specific areas of future technological staff development.

The survey determined the instructional applications of computers, the perceived technology needs of teachers to integrate computers into their classroom instruction, and whether the broad and general goals of the master plan to bring teachers to an awareness level of instructional computer use had been met.

Recommendations based upon the results of the survey were to be made with regard to the direction of future technological training for teachers, future technological support for teachers, and future purchases of equipment.

The Problem of Computer Integration Into the Classroom Curriculum

The district had previously inaugurated an educational master plan for infusing technology into the instructional program. The initial phase of staff development of the master plan, to bring teachers of the district to an awareness level of computer use, had been administered to teachers on a districtwide basis. Before moving into the second phase of the master plan, it was deemed necessary to assess the results of the initial phase of computer awareness of the teachers.

Like this district, many school districts have developed master plans for infusion of technology into the curriculum; however, unlike this district, the greater percentage of the school districts that have developed master plans for technology do not assess the success of the initial phase of the plan or they do not go beyond the awareness level of computer in-service. The expectation that teachers can fully and effectively integrate computers into their classroom instruction after a minimum of training and very little follow-up has not been realized.

As shown in chapter 2, there is little agreement as to what kind or how much training is necessary for teachers to integrate computers into the classroom curriculum successfully. Research also agrees that teachers must be directly involved in the planning of the programs. Unfortunately, the greater percentage of in-service technology programs are designed and planned top-down without adequate teacher input or follow-up.

Purpose of the Survey

A self-report questionnaire was designed to assess teachers' self-perceived needs for further technological training. This survey questionnaire was given to all teachers in the district. The results of the questionnaire were to be used by the District Technology Committee as a guide to design a program of technology use based on teachers' perceived needs.

The survey gathered information concerning the following areas: further technological staff development desired by teachers, teachers' perceived level of computer skills, and the computer strategies in which teachers would like to receive further training.

Questions around Which the Survey Was Framed

The survey questions were framed to gather specific information that focused on the above goals.

1. In which computer strategies do teachers desire more computer training?
2. In which areas do teachers use computers the greatest percentage of the time to support instruction?
3. At which levels of education (K-3, 4-6, 7-8, 9-12) do students use computers the greatest percentage of the time?
4. On a weekly basis, which teachers (classroom, resource teacher, special education) spend the greatest percentage of time utilizing computers in direct classroom instruction?
5. At which grade levels (K-3, 4-6, 7-8, 9-12) do the greatest percentage of teachers desire to receive more computer training?
6. At which grade levels do the greater percentage of teachers wish to improve their computer strategies in using software?
7. At which grade levels (K-3, 4-6, 7-8, 9-12) do teachers spend the greatest percentage of time in direct classroom instruction with computers?
8. At which level of computer skills (beginner, intermediate, advanced) do the greatest percentage of teachers perceive themselves to be?
9. In which ways do the greatest number of teachers utilize computers in their instruction: to introduce a lesson, for follow-up, to supplement, to reinforce a lesson, or to teach about computers?

Importance of the Survey

Although the survey was developed specifically for the District Technology Committee, the teachers of the district are a representative sample of classroom teachers. The primary importance of this questionnaire lies in the fact that it surveyed a significantly large number of classroom teachers concerning their instructional computer needs and their beliefs concerning those needs. A large population of teachers is represented in the results of this study. The district is part of the "magic circle" of Los Angeles County and Orange County, California, where multiethnic populations are represented in large numbers. The teachers of this district represent average or typical teachers; therefore, the results of the study should be generalizable to other teachers if the limitations of the survey are carefully considered.

It is important to note the limitations and the assumptions of this survey questionnaire. It is also important to note that the teachers surveyed had received computer awareness training that included an introduction to computers and a very basic hands-on keyboarding session.

Limitations of the Survey

- The survey was limited to the microcomputer.
- The teachers of the target district had previously received computer awareness training; therefore, the survey was designed to assess teachers who had previously received some computer training.
- The data collected were by self-report method. The accuracy of self-report information is difficult to establish.

Delimitations of the Survey

- The survey was limited to teachers of a specific district.
- Only the computer strategies and proficiencies designated by the Technology Committee were included in the survey.

Assumptions of the Survey

- That this district was a typical or average school district with teachers who represent "average" teachers.
- That respondents were able and willing to give truthful answers to the questionnaires. (All responses were anonymous.)

The long-range goal of the master plan for technology was for teachers to integrate technology use into their classroom curriculum based upon the teacher needs identified by the survey. However, the school district suffered serious budget constraints and the District Technology Committee was disbanded. Therefore, the master plan for technology and related activities were discontinued.

Chapter 10 of this book contains a summary and conclusions of the data acquired by the survey questionnaire. Using the data from this survey, chapter 11 offers computer strategies and student-centered activities appropriate for a whole class setting. Also, based upon the results of the questionnaire, chapter 13 offers a framework for school districts to use as a guide in developing in-service training programs for integrating technology into the classroom curriculum.

Chapter 10

THE O'DONNELL STUDY

The purpose of the survey was to assess teachers' level of computer skills and their needs for further computer training. Moreover, the survey determined in which specific areas teachers would like to receive computer training. The summaries and conclusions of the questionnaire are reported in this chapter. The first nine sections correspond to each of the nine questions identified in chapter 9. The most salient findings are discussed in relation to each of the questions. Following the survey questionnaire are sections on significant findings, implications, and recommendations for educators. The implications and recommendations section contains a discussion of the findings for school districts involved in staff development for the integration of computers into the instructional process.

1. In which computer strategies do teachers wish more computer training? (see also pp. 137-38)

The majority of the teachers wish to receive training in utilizing software for small-group cooperative learning activities. The second most desired software strategy is the utilization of software for individualized instruction. Using software for teacher-directed lessons was less desired, then editing/authoring computer software, and learning procedures for evaluating software for instructional use was the least desired computer strategy.

Teachers feel a lack of confidence in two of the most significant uses of computers in the classroom. Basic to computer use is the use of software. Two of the most important uses of computer software in instruction are the use of computers for small-group cooperative learning and for individualized instruction. Based on teachers' responses and on the importance of these areas, more training in these areas is warranted.

2. In which subject areas do teachers use computers the greatest percentage of the time to support instruction? (see also pp. 139-40)

Mathematics was the subject area that most utilized computers, but what was unexpected was the small percentage of teachers who utilize computers with their mathematics classes. Writing and reading were the subject areas that utilize computers the second most. In other subject areas, teachers' computer use was disappointing, with its lowest use found in the area of music. This can be partially understood when one considers the place of music in California schools. Many school districts have dropped all music teachers in grade levels K-8, with only high schools offering band practice and choirs.

Another surprising finding was that a very small percentage of the business education teachers utilize computers in their instruction. This is surprising because of the need for and the popularity of word processing programs. Science, mathematics, and health were also surprisingly low, although the areas of science and mathematics lend themselves very well to the use of computers.

The data indicate that, despite previous awareness training in computers, teachers are not sufficiently utilizing computers in their instruction. This is true even in subject areas that lend themselves to the use of computers.

3. At which levels of education, K-3, 4-6, 7-8, or 9-12, do students use computers the greatest percentage of time? (see also pp. 141-42)

One-quarter to two-fifths of the teachers reported that the greatest percentage of time spent by students on computers in the classroom is at the 4-6 and K-3 grade levels, and it is only 15-29 minutes per week. The lowest percentage of time that students spend using computers in their classroom instruction on a weekly basis was at the grade 7-8 and 9-12 levels, where at least half of the teachers report that students spend no time using computers in the classroom.

These data clearly show that students in grades K-6 spend more time per week in their classroom on computers than do those in grades 7-12. This may indicate that teachers of grade levels 7-12 are not utilizing computers to their fullest extent.

4. On a weekly basis, which teachers (classroom teachers, resource teachers, or special education teachers) spend the greatest percentage of time utilizing computers in direct classroom instruction? (see also pp.143-44)

The greatest percentage of computer usage in direct classroom instruction was found among the resource teachers, with one-quarter responding that they use computers in direct classroom instruction for more than one hour on a weekly basis.

These findings indicate that although computers are used in the classroom, they are not an integral component of regular classroom instruction. Computer use remains peripheral to the instructional process.

5. At which grade levels do the greatest percentage of teachers wish to receive more computer training? (see also pp. 145-58)

Approximately two-thirds of teachers at the K-3 level would like training to improve their personal computer skills. This parallels the findings for Question 3 that teachers in the lower grades utilize computers a greater percentage of the time than do teachers in grades 9-12. As such, they are more likely to be concerned with their skills. However, over half of 7-12 grade teachers also indicated an interest in improving personal computer skills.

At each grade level, a different computer skill is listed as the most desired skill in which to receive future training. This finding indicates that teachers at each grade level have different computer needs. This factor has not been addressed in staff training programs of the past and may be a major factor in the failure to have computers integrated into the instructional program.

6. At which grade levels do the greatest percentage of teachers wish to improve their computer strategies in using software? (see also pp. 159-75)

An important aspect of this survey was to assess at which grade levels teachers wish to receive training in utilizing software. Previous research indicates that evaluation of software is a very important skill in the integration of computers into the instructional process at all grade levels. However, that was not found here. Teachers preferred to receive training in the actual classroom use of the software and not in the evaluation process. The greatest percentage of teachers at the K-3, 4-6, and 9-12 grade levels wished to receive computer training in using software for small-group cooperative learning situations. However, these findings may not be appropriate to teachers who have not received previous in-service at the computer awareness level.

Teachers at different grade levels wish to receive training in different software strategies. However, greatest interest in using software for small-group cooperative learning is seen at the 4-6, K-3, and the 9-12 grade levels. Using software for individual instruction was the second most desired computer strategy among these same teachers.

7. At which grade level (K-3, 4-6, 7-8, 9-12) do teachers spend the greatest percentage of time in direct classroom instruction with computers? (see also pp. 176-77)

The greatest percentage of computer usage is at the 9-12 grade level. However, the amount of usage is small in that less than one fifth of teachers utilize computers one hour or more per week. The least amount of computer use is among teachers at the K-3 and 7-8 grade levels, where over two-thirds of teachers do not use computers at all. Among grades 9-12, just less than two-thirds of teachers report no computer use. These results indicate that even after teachers have received basic computer awareness in-service training, they still are not sufficiently utilizing computers in their classroom instruction. Using Question 3 as a cross reference, it seems that computer use is low for teachers and students at all grade levels.

8. At which level of computer skills (beginner, intermediate, advanced) do the greatest percentage of teachers perceive themselves to be? (see also pp. 178-79)

Less than one-tenth of the classroom teachers perceive them-selves to be at the advanced level of computer skills, while over half perceive themselves to be at the beginner level. Research has shown that many teachers have problems in assessing their own level of computer skill. However, it remains important to know at what level the teachers believe they are functioning, because this belief will influence their use of computers. These findings reinforce previous research that has found that teachers are often ill-prepared to utilize computers in the instructional process.

9. In which ways do the greatest number of teachers utilize computers in their instruction? (see also pp. 180-81)

The greatest percentage of computer use involves supplementing lessons. This reinforces the finding that computer use is not an integral part of the instructional process. Teachers utilize computers about a third of the time to reinforce lessons and less than one-fifth of the time to introduce lessons. No teachers utilized computers as an integral part of the lesson. Finally, only a fifth of the teachers utilize computers to teach about computers. Clearly, teachers need to learn how to make computers an integral part of classroom instruction. The results show that not only has an awareness level been achieved, but over one-half of teachers wish to receive further training in instructional computing. Because the percentage of teachers who utilize computers in the classroom is low, the instructional use of computers is not fully integrated into the instructional process.

However, many teachers utilize computers for supplementing or reinforcing lessons. This would indicate that although computer use is low and not fully integrated into the instructional process, computers are utilized for instructional purposes. Another important finding is that the majority of teachers believe that they are at the beginner level of computer use. This finding is significant because teachers tend to function at the level at which they perceive their computer skills to be.

Summary of Questions 1-9

The results show a relationship between grade level and instructional computer use. There were four grade level groupings (K-3, 4-6, 6-8, and 9-12) and four time frames (1-14 minutes, 15-29 minutes, 30-59 minutes, and 60 minutes or more) over a one-week period. Students in grades K-3 were more likely to utilize computers in their classrooms than were students in grade levels 7-12. However, even in grades K-3, the amount of time that students spent on a weekly basis with computers was only 15-29 minutes. Computer use by teachers in direct classroom instruction was highest at the 9-12 grade levels, with only 1 percent of K-3 teachers responding that they utilized computers in direct classroom instruction. The greatest amount of time that teachers or students spent in the classroom on computers is 15-29 minutes. This finding may imply that computers are utilized in a different manner at different grade levels or that computer use in K-3 grade level is less integrated into the classroom instruction than at the 9-12 grade level.

Perceived Technology Needs of Teachers

The majority of teachers believed that they were at the beginning level of computer use. Teachers at the elementary level may be able to utilize computers in their instruction more readily than teachers at the higher grade levels because students at the lower grade levels are also at the beginning levels of computer use. In turn, teachers at the higher grade levels may require more advanced computer skills. They may need to redesign their instruction to incorporate computers into the instruction because the students have more advanced computer skills and the subject matter is more advanced.

Computer Skills, Computer Uses, and Instructional Strategies

The most preferred instructional strategy among teachers was utilizing software for small-group cooperative learning. Using software for individual instructional use was the second most preferred instructional strategy. The least preferred strategy was evaluating software for student use. This finding is significant because much emphasis has been placed on the evaluation of software. Teachers may feel confident in selecting software for student use, but they do not always feel confident in the instructional use of computer software. The instructional utilization of software for student use requires the development and design of appropriate instruction to utilize the software in the classroom.

K-3 teachers were the largest majority wishing to receive training in utilizing software for small group cooperative learning. Utilizing software for individualized instructional settings was the second most desired computer strategy for teachers in all grade levels and was almost evenly distributed across K-12. Using software for teacher-directed lessons was only slightly more desired at the K-3 level than at the 7-12 level. More than half of all teachers wished for further training in this area, and interest increased as the grade level increased.

There are several ways to interpret these findings. One interpretation is that teachers do not feel confident in utilizing computers in direct classroom instruction at all grade levels. Another interpretation is that different uses for computers are required at the different grade levels and that different computer strategies are appropriate at the different grade levels.

Significant Findings

Expectations that the majority of teachers would utilize computers in direct classroom instruction have not been realized. Educators have failed to recognize the trends that have been highlighted by past and current research. Teachers have become overwhelmed with the rapid placement of computers into classrooms. Research has emphasized that the integration of computers into the instructional process is a slow and ongoing process, but one that can be facilitated with appropriate teacher training and support.

One significant finding of this survey is that the majority of teachers do not understand how to use computers in the teaching process, to utilize software, or to redesign their instruction to incorporate computers into the classroom instruction. The majority of teachers also do not understand how to use computers with students in actual classroom instructional situations, such as small-group cooperative learning, individualized instruction, and teacher-directed learning situations, which are basic to the integration of computers into the instructional process.

Another significant finding of this survey is the manner in which computers are being used in the classroom. The result that teachers desire training in classroom instructional situations, small-group cooperative learning situations, individualized instruction, and teacher-directed learning situations indicates that computers are not being utilized in a manner that is basic to the instructional process.

The data from this study strongly suggest that teachers at different levels of education not only desire different computer skills and strategies but need different skills in order to integrate computers into the classroom. The results of the survey indicate that teachers are ill-prepared for instructional computer use. Moreover, the integration of computers into the classroom is an ongoing process that consists of a multiplicity of interrelated factors including grade level, subject area, teacher perceptions, and teacher skills.

Implications for Educators

It is important to know teachers' perceptions of their computer skills and the extent of their desire to receive further training. Results of this research imply that teachers do desire to utilize computers in their instruction but lack the computer skills, instructional strategies, and the general technical knowledge to do so. They also lack the knowledge to restructure their classroom instruction to integrate computers into the instructional process.

This book emphasizes that staff development programs must be formulated around the specific needs of teachers and that staff development sessions should be designed to be ongoing over an extended period of time. The results of this research have shown that it is impossible for integration of computers into classrooms to happen quickly. Educators mistakenly expected that the integration of computers into the instructional process would occur if the hardware, the software, and a minimum of guidance and staff development programs were offered to teachers. However, this has not been the case. The integration of computers into instruction is a complex process, with a multiplicity of factors which occur over a long period of time. If instructional computer use is to reach its full potential, educators cannot ignore specific teacher needs. It is evident from the teacher responses to the O'Donnell survey concerning computer classroom strategies, computer skills, and further training that teachers desire to utilize computers in their classrooms but do not know how. In addition, it is important to restructure staff development programs to understand the craft culture of teaching and to design objectives around teachers' identified needs.

It is important for school district administrators and college of education professors to understand the manner in which computers are being used in the classroom, the needs of the teachers who would be integrating computers, and what levels of computer skills the teachers possess. Such information can provide direction for the design of in-service training programs, research programs, and the preservice training of prospective classroom teachers.

School districts should design, develop, and administer technological staff-development training programs based upon classroom teachers' identified computer needs. Based upon the results of this survey, school district instructional design technologists should design in-service training for the integration of computers into the instructional process not only in relation to the needs of the teachers, but also by broad general grade levels (K-3, 4-6, 7-8, 9-12). The results of this survey also indicate a strong need to train teachers in the student-centered strategies that allow teachers to redesign their instructional program of classroom teaching to integrate computers into the instructional process. In this manner, much of the trial and error of computer in-service training can be prevented, thus saving school districts significant amounts of money while realizing their goals of integrating computers into classroom instruction.

Recommendations for Educators

The recommendations in this book are based upon the highly complex nature of integrating computers into instruction, the multiplicity of factors involved in that process, and the recognition that teaching is a creative craft and not a technical culture. These recommendations require the identification of specific factors involved in the instructional use of computers.

The first recommendation would require a change in philosophy that has been prevalent in past staff-development programs that computer integration can become a reality with a minimum of preservice and in-service training. A major recommendation of this book is that funds be allocated by school districts to employ a degreed instructional design technologist to develop and design staff development programs that specifically address teachers' ongoing needs of acquiring computer strategies and computer skills and that support teachers as they move from traditional methods of instruction to a wholistic integration of computers into the classroom. The third recommendation is that designers of staff development programs recognize that computer integration does not happen quickly and that the majority of teachers desire to integrate computers into their daily classroom instruction but do not know how.

In addition, expenditures for staff development should include categorical funds for an instructional design technologist at the district level to design and develop staff development programs for computer integration that move from a hands-on computer focus to a focus on the instruction that is to be imparted to the students by the teacher.

The instructional design technologist will provide the sustained assistance that enables teachers to restructure their classroom instruction to employ teaching methods and strategies to incorporate computers into their classroom instruction. The survey strongly indicates that educators must become aware of the multiplicity of factors that are inherent in the integration of computers into the instructional process.

Chapter 11

INSTRUCTIONAL STRATEGIES
AND IN-SERVICE PLANS

The results of the survey reveal that teachers wish to utilize computers in their classrooms. However, the majority of them do not understand how to use computers in the teaching process, to utilize software, or to design their instruction to integrate computers into classroom instruction. Teachers also do not understand how to use computers in classroom instructional situations, such as small-group cooperative learning, individualized instruction, and teacher-directed learning situations. These pedagogical methods are basic to the integration of computers into the instructional process. A new and different approach to the in-service of classroom teachers for integrating computers into instruction is suggested by the results of the survey.

This revised approach to preservice and in-service focuses on the teacher, the key to computer integration, whose needs must be targeted and met. A focus on the needs of classroom teachers will serve to carry the message that their needs are important and will serve as the catalyst for enthusiastic participation in in-service sessions. The plans in this book acknowledge the specific identified needs of the classroom teacher as the primary key to the integration of computers into the classroom. These plans will enable school districts to design, develop, and administer training programs based upon the identified classroom needs of teachers.

Educators must become aware of the multiplicity of factors that are inherent in the integration of computers into the instructional process before designing in-service programs. It is also important for administrators and principals to understand the manner in which computers are being used in the classroom, the needs of teachers who would be integrating computers, and what level of computer skills the teachers possess. This book clarifies some of the factors involved in designing in-service programs and provides the keys to enabling educators to design effective in-service programs that meet the needs of teachers.

Teachers at different levels of education not only desire different computer skills and strategies, but require different skills in order to integrate computers into the classroom. Moreover, teachers do not

89

understand how to restructure their classroom curriculum to integrate computers into the instructional process. The keys to computer integration found in this book are based upon the highly complex nature of integrating computers into instruction, the multiplicity of factors involved in that process, and the recognition that teaching is a craft culture, not a technical culture. This book also emphasizes that in-service programs should be formulated around the instructional needs of the teachers of the district and designed to cover an extended period of time. It is impossible to expect the integration of computers into instruction to happen quickly.

Following are instructional strategies and brief suggestions for preservice and in-service training based upon the results of the survey. The instructional strategies and suggestions are intended as examples from which districts and colleges of education can frame training programs to meet the unique needs of the teachers who are to participate in the training.

The Questionnaire

The survey questionnaire for this study appears in Appendix A. The questionnaire was framed around the questions listed in chapter 9. The first section of the questionnaire, Questions 1 through 6, solicits demographic information. This section was designed to obtain data concerning areas of education in which teachers worked, the grade levels taught, and the school site at which computers were being used. The second section, Questions 7-20, is concerned with the computer training of the teachers. These questions pertain to personal use of the computer and computer strategies appropriate for the classroom. Reported are the areas in which teachers would like to improve computer skills to utilize computers in their classroom instruction, areas in which they would like to receive additional computer training, and teachers' self-reported competency levels. This section is the focus of this chapter.

The third section, Questions 21-52, covers the actual computer use of the teachers. It gathers data on the number of computers currently used by students in their instruction and assesses the time students spend using computers in the classroom and the time teachers spend using computers in direct classroom instruction. This section also gathers data on the ways and subject areas in which computers are being used in the classroom. The results appear in Appendix B.

Summary of the Survey and Suggestions for Teacher In-Service Programs

This section presents suggestions based upon the findings of the survey, regarding how teachers can easily integrate computers in their classroom instruction. Each survey question is stated with the accompanying results. Specific teaching strategies related to each survey question are followed by recommendations for designing in-service training directed at the results of that particular survey question.

It is important to note that all suggestions are directed toward a whole class situation in a self-contained classroom. Class size may vary from perhaps 20 to 40 students. The teacher will probably have only one computer in the classroom and may have none at all. It may be necessary for the teacher to move the class to a computer lab or a library media technology center to have access to a computer. These suggestions are valid in any type of situation. Ideally, the teacher will have access to enough computers that half of the class can work on a computer simultaneously. A cost-effective way of providing a whole class access to computers is to provide teachers with a computer and monitor and to provide each pair of students with a laptop or a powerbook. These guidelines are constructed for a one-or-more computer format, depending upon the classroom situation of the teacher.

Question 1: In Which Computer Strategies Do Teachers Wish More Computer Training?

The majority of teachers wish to receive training in instructional strategies which utilize software in a whole class setting, with small-group cooperative learning activities, and with teacher-directed lessons. Each of these instructional strategies will be addressed in pages 92-102.

Whole Class Setting

It is important to note that not all students will respond to an instructional strategy in the same way. Slower students may need more direction in how to use the computer. Hativa found that the slower students may not be as able as the faster learners to make the switch from paper and pencil to computers, even with user-friendly drill and practice programs. Hativa also found that computer practice seems to be more profitable for the more able learners. Hativa believes that the higher-achieving students are more prone to seek teacher assistance than the lower-achieving students, who are less flexible in their ability to adjust to a new situation.[1]

Teacher strategies should always include close monitoring of both individuals and groups while they are working at the computer, especially the slower students. Teachers should assign students to computers by pairing the lower achievers with the higher achievers so they can assist the slower students. Carrier and Sales found that students who work in pairs seem to spend more time on practice items and on inspecting the menu for feedback types than do students who work on an individual basis. They also found that students who work in pairs are more likely to choose the more elaborate feedback options.[2]

Teachers should monitor students closely while being alert to anyone who may be having difficulties. Teachers should rotate to each group and among individual students to diagnose and clarify the acquisitions of concepts to be learned. They should always allow adequate reinforcement and practice time. The software should be matched with student need and lesson requirements. Various types of software should be available so that students may be to assigned to the most appropriate software for their individual needs.

It is important to show teachers how to respond to common error messages when utilizing software. They should be given a demonstration of the lesson utilizing each type of software. They should also have ample time to work through each lesson that they will be using in the classroom. Special attention should be given to the instructional strategies that are appropriate for each type of software, and the instructional support available should be explained.

Utilizing Software for Small Group Cooperative Learning

Before assigning any student to the computer in a whole class setting, the teacher should review the objectives of the lesson with the class and discuss the total content of the lesson, with emphasis on what is to be learned during each class session. Each step in the lesson should be explained and demonstrated. The software should be named and an explanation given of how it relates to the lesson. While utilizing a large-screen monitor, the teacher should demonstrate how the software is to be used. Research shows that two students to a computer is optimal.[3] However, if there is only one computer available, the teacher should assign a shorter time period on the computer for each pair of students or assign three students to a computer. A student who is familiar with the computer should be paired with a student who is not familiar with the computer, or a faster learner should be paired with a slower learner. Each group should know the rotation order and how much time is alloted on the computer.

The teacher should inform students that while the groups are on the computer, other students will be busy with related activities at their seats. The teacher should also explain that the related activities are important to the instruction and that each student is responsible for the seat work as well as the work on the computer. If the students are unfamiliar with computers, the teacher should distribute a drawing of the keyboard and have students locate the keys they will be using for the lesson. Each step in the computer lesson activity should be demonstrated while having students follow on their paper keyboards. Students should be instructed to choose a partner, or a partner should be assigned to each student. They should be given an instruction sheet that summarizes the activity that they will be doing. They should be reminded of the rotation format and how much time they have with each part of the activity. An instruction sheet should be taped beside each computer. The teacher should be alert to any students who may need help. When all students have finished the activity, the teacher and class should discuss the lesson, with the teacher asking for and fielding questions to determine understanding.

Teacher-Directed Lessons

Unless there is a computer for each student, the use of computers in a whole class setting will involve the rotation of students from computer to seat. This rotation process requires a certain amount of time. Therefore, the teacher should organize the instruction in a time-effective manner so that there is time to have a class demonstration, discuss ideas, clarify concepts, and assign homework. In whole class instructional situations, computers with a large-screen monitor can serve as a demonstration aid for imparting concepts and ideas. Software that creates an interactive mode between teacher, student, and computer is an appropriate model that has a powerful instructional impact.[4]

This type of teacher and whole class interaction requires a large-screen monitor to focus and amplify class development of ideas about concepts and theories for whole class viewing and discussion. The teacher should ask the class to predict each step of the concept and then, by utilizing the computer, provide an animated display of the particular idea inherent in the concept. This animation can be repeated as often as needed. Teachers can then choose options relating to the practical application of the concept in specific instructional situations.

The use of computers in an interactive whole class discussion can often be more instructionally effective than interaction with a single student at a computer. An interactive whole class mode is also more time effective than the rotation of students from seat to computer, especially if there is only one computer in the class. The teacher, utilizing a large-screen demonstration monitor in a whole class mode, can clarify concepts and relationships with animation, movement, and sound in a time-effective manner. Computers can then be used to reinforce concepts on an individual basis.

Computer use in the classroom should be a response to an instructional need. The teaching strategies employed with computers should be appropriate to the grade level, the instructional goals, and the specific needs of the students.

How to Address In-Service Training

To address teacher concerns, districts should develop in-service training by specific grade levels for elementary teachers. At the secondary level in-service groups should be formed around academic subject areas, such as mathematics, science, or social studies. In-service should not be approached in a general manner with large numbers of teachers in attendance. Rather, small groups, such as subject area departments, or grade levels should form a group. In this manner, teachers will feel that a personal interest is being taken in their professional skills, and their specific instructional concerns can be addressed in a valid manner. When in-service is approached in a manner that does not answer instructional needs, teachers may develop an increasingly negative view of computers in instruction. Addressing teacher needs should be the primary concern when designing staff development programs for instructional computer use.

At both the elementary and the secondary levels, student-centered instructional strategies utilizing computers should be the focus of the information imparted. Training in utilizing software in student-centered instructional situations with the textbook and other teaching materials should be the primary emphasis of the sessions.

Teacher concerns regarding student-centered whole class instructional strategies should be of the utmost concern for those persons who are responsible for designing and developing preservice or in-service training for the integration of computers into the classroom. Instructional computer strategies should include the most successful manner in which to introduce and impart concepts and to reinforce instruction. Teachers also need to be shown appropriate uses for computers in curriculum-related activities and how to easily utilize computers without changing their teaching strategies or their classroom environment in an extreme manner.

Teachers should receive a complete lesson plan including appropriate instructional strategies to employ in a whole class setting. Teachers should also be advised where they may check out the software with complete lesson plans and instructions for the use of the software in a whole class setting with small groups or individual students. Enough hardware and software should be available so that each teacher can have adequate practical hands-on time. Teachers should be provided with the time and the assistance to become familiar with all hardware and software with which they are provided.

Teachers need to understand the most successful manner in which to introduce and to utilize software in a classroom situation. All in-service training should allow classroom teachers to experience working with software in the context of the curriculum. No in-service activities should be conducted in isolation or removed from classroom curriculum objectives.

Question 2: In Which Subject Areas Do Teachers Use Computers the Greatest Percentage of the Time to Support Instruction?

Computers were most utilized in the subject areas of mathematices, writing, and reading. Computer use was low in business and science. This finding is surprising because of the usefulness of computers in offices and laboratories. Instructional strategies for mathematices, reading and writing, science and business are addressed on pages 96-102.

Instructional Strategies: Mathematics

A general strategy for a whole class mathematics setting is to review previous material and then introduce the concepts to be learned. The instructional objectives of the lesson should be clearly stated. The mathematics concepts to be learned should be demonstrated utilizing a computer and a large-screen monitor. The teacher should discuss and clarify the mathematics concepts, with students verbalizing the concept, then writing the concept in their own words. In a class discussion, with students helping, the teacher should translate the concept to numbers. The teacher should demonstrate the software program in a whole class setting using a large-screen monitor while explaining how the software is to be used. Before allowing students to go to a computer, the teacher should give them a set of written instructions to clarify what they are to do. After computer time, each student should be given a fact sheet explaining the mathematics concept illustrated with problems to practice. In a whole class setting, the teacher should go over the practice problems while reviewing and discussing the concepts that are to be learned.

In-service Training: Mathematics

Acquaint teachers with mathematics software, tutorials, drill and practice, problem solving, critical thinking, and games. Also, acquaint teachers with the software that best focuses on each mathematics concept, such as addition, subtraction, multiplication, problem solving, and sets. Explain the differences between the different types of software, noting for which instructional situation each is best suited. Explain the limitations of each type of software. Demonstrate the use of each type of software, while utilizing instructional strategies appropriate for a whole class environment and explaining each type of teaching strategy used. Speak to the importance of assessment strategy for mathematics students to confirm that the concept has been understood. Teachers should be given written sample lesson plans illustrating the mathematics concept to be taught, the appropriate type of software to use, and the teaching strategies that are most appropriate.

Instructional Strategies: Reading and Writing

Clement states that computers may have a profound impact on children's learning in the language arts.[5] It seems that teachers agree with Clement because the most preferred computer skill of teachers in grades K-3 was how to use word processing programs in their classroom. Interesting instructional potential exists for computers in reading and writing instruction that involves an interaction between teacher, student, and computer that merges all three into a cohesive unit not possible before. However, facility in word processing does not come in a short time period, but develops gradually with repeated opportunities for use.[6] Other limitations to the use of word processing programs for instructional use are a lack of hardware, limited student keyboarding skills, and student lack of familiarity with a word processing program.[7]

The following strategies are useful in a whole class setting where only one or possibly two computers are available. These strategies are designed so that each student will have equal time on the computer. The necessary equipment is a computer, a printer, and a word processing program. The teacher will have an opportunity to exercise creativity and to individualize learning by developing exercises for the unique abilities of the students. These basic suggestions may be expanded into other more sophisticated areas of reading and writing, as the teacher and students feel confident.

Initially the teacher should prepare a master file on disk of exercises in the lesson illustrating the concepts the class will be learning. In a whole class setting, the objectives of the lesson should be explained. Students should be assigned to the computers in pairs.[8] If possible, a high achiever and a low achiever should be paired, or a student who knows how to use a computer should be paired with a student who does not know how to use the computer.[9]

In a whole class setting, utilizing a large-screen monitor, the concepts to be learned should be demonstrated, and each point assessed for student understanding. If students are unfamiliar with the keyboard, a paper keyboard should be distributed to each student with the keys that they will use marked in red. The red keys should be brought to the students' attention while explaining what each key will do when it is depressed. Students should be shown how to prepare a disk, how to load and unload it, and how to save their data.

While utilizing a large-screen demonstration monitor, the teacher should have the students come to the computer in pairs, load the disk, perform the exercise, and then save the work on the disk. As students perform their task, the teacher should discuss the concept, utilizing their work as an instructional example for the class. If a printer is available, the teacher should print a copy of the exercise for each pair of students. After each pair of students has completed the exercise and saved their work, the teacher should have them unload the disk in preparation for the next pair of students. After each pair of students has rotated to the computer, the teacher should discuss the lesson and the operation of the computer with the students, while clarifying any misconceptions they may have about the computer or the lesson. If no printer is available, the teacher should distribute a previously prepared copy of the exercise to the students and have them make corrections on the paper copy. The teacher should instruct students to take their work home to share with family and friends.

In-Service Training: Reading and Writing

Teachers need to understand the types of software available for reading and writing instruction. The instructional design technologist should explain each type of software (word processing, skill oriented, and drill and practice) while pointing out the differences between them and explaining the instructional activities for which each is most appropriate. Teachers need to know how best to use each type of software in a classroom setting with the instructional strategies that are best suited for small group-centered and individual instruction with each type of software. The instructional design technologist should also demonstrate how to turn the computer on and off and how to load each program. How to connect the printer, how to fill the paper tray, and how to print an assignment should also be demonstrated. Teachers should be shown how to work through a whole class demonstration of a typical lesson, utilizing a computer, a large-screen monitor, and a printer with each type of software. Teachers should also receive an explanation of whole class instructional strategies that are appropriate for each type of software. Each teacher should be given an opportunity to perform each function. Teachers should receive a sample lesson plan that includes specific classroom strategies framed around each type of software they will be utilizing in their classrooms. The software programs should be distributed with the lesson plans that teachers are to utilize. All software and all lesson plans should be available upon demand for teachers who wish to utilize them in their classroom.

Instructional Strategies: Business

All business teachers should have a computer lab with enough computers so that each student has a computer to work with during class time. The two most common types of computers in industry are IBM compatibles and Macintosh. These two brands should be represented in all business classes and loaded with at least two of the programs that are most commonly used in the work place.

Students should be given a manual containing the points that they are to learn during the lesson. While students follow in the manual, the teacher should explain each point in the lesson. The teacher should give full instructional objectives, while explaining what students are to learn from the lesson. The teacher should be certain that each student understands, and if not, the teacher should clarify any misconceptions. The teacher should demonstrate on the computer, utilizing a large-screen monitor, what students are to learn and the appropriate computer functions. Students should be shown specifically what they are to do, and must be given ample hands-on practice time on the computer. The teacher should circulate around the classroom, being alert to any problem area that students may have and giving immediate feedback. All questions should be answered and demonstrated on the computer, while making certain that students understand.

In-Service Training: Business

The instructional design technologist should explain each type of software that the teacher will be using and demonstrate the teaching strategies that teachers will utilize with the software. The importance of utilizing the computer and a large-screen monitor during the instructional period should be emphasized. Teachers should be cautioned not to rely only on the lecture and manual method. A focus on the interaction of the teacher, the student, and the computer in a classroom setting should be emphasized. The specific whole class strategies that teachers should employ with the software should be demonstrated, and a sample lesson plan showing the appropriate instructional strategies to utilize with students should be distributed.

The availability of teacher support before, during, and after class should be stressed.

Instructional Strategies: Science

Currently, the philosophy underlying good science is that science experiences in the classroom should replicate the application of a scientific approach to real life situations.[10] Students should also be offered the opportunity to work with the technological tools of science.[11] Even if there is only one computer in the classroom, computers can enable teachers to help students achieve the intended goals by utilizing the computer with a large-screen monitor.

Initially, students should be assigned to the computer in pairs. Students who are high achievers or who are computer literate should be distributed among the groups. In a whole class demonstration, utilizing a large-screen color monitor, the teacher should explain the concept to be learned. A paper worksheet diagram of the concept should be distributed to each student. Students should be directed to focus attention on the diagram while the teacher explains the important aspects of the lesson. Questions should be fielded to confirm that the students understand the concept.

Utilizing a large-screen color monitor, the teacher should have the class observe an animated illustration while explaining the concept in its entirety and focusing on the interrelated movements and actions of the various parts. Each pair of students should be directed to use the demonstration computer as a work station while the teacher explains the actions and interrelations in the concept to be learned. Each pair of students should be directed to manipulate the demonstration software in the manner requested by the teacher, while the students at their desks watch and trace the action of the concept on their paper diagram. The teacher should have the students at their desks color in the proper color with crayons or colored pencils, such as red for the blood stream, for each portion of the concept that is being taught, as it is shown on the computer monitor.

When the class activity is completed and all students have had an opportunity to manipulate the computer demonstration, the teacher should field questions to confirm that all students understand the concept. Students should be challenged with questions that indicate the ability to transfer the concept to new situations. The teacher should instruct the class to take the diagram home to share with family and friends.

In-Service Training: Science

With complete cooperation at the district level, teachers should decide which hardware and software are needed to enhance science education, how a computer will improve the process of teaching, and the basic instructional strategies they wish to acquire in order to use computers in the science classroom.

Before undertaking the in-service of science teachers, the equipment must be available in the classroom. The school district should provide at least one computer with large-screen capability in each science classroom. The in-service training should encompass ways in which the integration of computers into a whole class environment with one or more computers in the classroom can be accomplished.

Teachers should be acquainted with the different types of science software programs, such as simulations, and microcomputer based laboratories (MBL) that are available for the science classroom. All science teachers should be instructed in how to utilize these programs with appropriate classroom strategies. Science teachers should be introduced to interactive video/computer programs such as CD-ROM and interactive video and laser disc programs gradually as they are ready for them. The differences in each type of software, the instructional applications that each is most appropriate for, and the instructional strategies to be employed with each type of software should be explained by the instructional design technologist. The improved impact on learning that the appropriate instructional support by the teacher gives, such as specific guidance before, during, and after the use of the computer, should be emphasized.

The instructional design technologist should demonstrate the use of MBLs for data collection as an experiment progresses, how to save the data, how to display the data, and how to print it for analysis as it would be used in a whole class setting. Ellis and Keurbis believe that teachers should understand the use of the computer as an instructional tool in the classroom and know how to integrate the use of the computer with non-computer materials, such as textbooks and interactive videos.[12]

Ellis and Keurbis also believe this should include knowledge of the software, the peripherals interfaced with laboratory apparatus for collection of laboratory data, simple data bases for electronic storage of data, graphing programs for analysis, and use of the computer as a demonstration tool.[13] They also state that in-service for science teachers should include the computer competencies that emphasize computers as a tool for science classroom instruction[14]

Yeany and Padilla believe that modeling has proved successful in changing teacher behavior.[15] An effective manner of changing teacher behavior is to provide videotapes as a demonstration model showing teachers utilizing computers successfully in the science classroom.[16] Appropriate follow-up to science in-service is to have an instructional technologist available for classroom visits to assist teachers until they feel comfortable and confident with the hardware and the software.

Notes

1. N. Hativa, "Computer-based Drill and Practice in Arithmetic: Widening the Gap Between High and Low Achieving Students." *American Educational Research Journal* 25, no. 3 (1988): 366-397.

2. C. Carrier and G. Sales, "Pair vs. Individual Work on the Acquisition of Concepts in a Computer Based Instructional Lesson" *Journal of Computer Based Instruction* 14, no. 1 (1987): 11-17.

3. Ibid.

4. N. Hativa, "Teacher-Student-Computer Interaction: An Application That Enhances Teacher Effectiveness," in *Computers In Mathematics Education: 1984 Yearbook* (V. P. Hansen and M. Z. Zwegg, Reston, VA: National Council Teachers of Mathematics, 1984): 89-96.

5. D. Clement, *Computers in Early and Primary Education* (Englewood Cliffs, NJ: Prentice-Hall, 1985): 191.

6. B. Dalton, C. Morocco, and A. Neale, "I've Lost My Story!" Mastering the Machine Skills for Word Processing " (paper presented at the annual meeting of the American Educational Research Association New Orleans, LA. 1988); B. Collis, *Computers, Curriculum, and Whole-Class Instruction: Issues and Idea* (Belmont CA, Wadsworth Publishing Company, 1988): 135.

7. Ibid.
8. Carrier and Sales, "Pair vs. Individual."
9. Hativa, "Teacher-Student-Computer Interaction."
10. B. Kahn, *Computers in Science: Using Computers for Learning and Teaching* (Cambridge, England: Cambridge University Press, 1985): 8.
11. Ibid.
12. J. Ellis and P. Keurbis, "Development and Validation of Essential Computer Literacy Competencies for Science Teachers" (paper presented at the Annual Meeting of the Association for Research in Science Teaching, French Lick, Indiana, 1985): 22.
13. Ibid.
14. Ibid.
15. R. Yeany and M. Padilla, "Training Science Teachers to Use Better Teaching Strategies," *Journal of Research in Science Teaching* 2, no. 2 (1986): 85-96.
16. Ibid. See also M. Fullan, M. Miles, and S. Anderson, *Strategies for Implementation of Microcomuters in Schools: The Ontario Case* (Toronto, Ontario: Ministry of Education, 1987).

Chapter 12

SOFTWARE RECOMMENDATIONS FOR TEACHERS

The results of the survey conducted by O'Donnell show that the instructional strategy most desired by teachers is how to utilize software in small-group cooperative learning situations. The second most desired instructional strategy is utilizing software in individual learning situations, and the third is using software for teacher-directed lessons.[1] The results of the survey also show that the subject areas that most utilize the computer in instruction are mathematics, reading, and writing. Business and science are also basic academic areas and as such will be considered in the following information on how to utilize software programs.

Mathematics was the subject area that most utilized computers; however, instructional computer use was disappointingly low. Writing and reading utilized instructional computers the second most, but again, the use was low. It should be noted that teacher-perceived needs for in-service training coupled with a lack of instructional computer use in the classroom indicates a lack of confidence in utilizing conputers in a whole class environment. These findings also indicate that teachers do not understand how to utilize software in an instructional situation. More importantly, however, these findings indicate that teachers realize what that they need to know, that is, how to use instructional software in a whole class setting, which is primary to the integration of computers into the classroom.

For ease of selection, all software should be previewed for teachers. A list of appropriate quality software should be circulated to teachers on a regular basis. A software and preview center should be established at each school library media technology center where teachers can become personally familiar with each software program before using it in the classroom. All software should be curriculum related and accompanied with teacher instructional packages that include lesson plans and teacher-directed student instructional packages.

Mathematics Software

There is more software published in mathematics than in any other subject area; however, the majority of the software for mathematics are drill and practice programs. Hativa believes that drill and practice should be used with caution because of their many limitations.[2] Hativa also believes that teachers may not be aware of the specific problems that the student misses and that students may become bored or frustrated with the repetitive nature of the program and may not have a clear idea of what they are doing wrong. However, Hativa believes that when compared to teacher worksheets, drill and practice software is the more effective for student learning. Hativa also found that drill and practice software that offer branching programs and a variety of exercises with immediate feedback for students are effective to reinforce learning.

Hativa indicates that mathematics drill and practice programs that offer animation and sound are the most effective, because basic math facts and skills are learned through repetition and reinforcement. In addition, Hativa found that if the program is interesting students are more likely to stay in a practice mode longer.[3] Whether it is a teacher-prepared worksheet or a computer program, repetitive practice is boring for students; however, drill and practice software will offer the student a certain amount of interaction with the computer.[6]

Bozeman and Burns reviewed forty studies where teachers were using mathematics drill and practice programs and found that there were significant gains for students on computers as opposed to students in a traditional classroom with worksheets. They also indicate that drill and practice programs are quite successful when used only for repetitive basic skills study, and for a short length of time or until the student tires.[4]

The research, however, is inconclusive. There are studies that cite significant gains with the use of drill and practice programs, and there are studies that find no significant gains. Hativa cautions the teacher to be aware of the lower-achieving students who may need careful monitoring of their progress when using a computer drill and practice program.[5] Hativa also believes that mathematics teachers should approach computer software use with caution. Instructional software should be carefully evaluated and assessed for instructional effectiveness.

Computer software choices should be driven by the instructional objectives of the lesson for which the software is to be used. In mathematics at grade levels K-12, there are basic concepts that students must learn. An understanding of these concepts develops through sensory and manipulative experiences.[6] Literally hundreds of commercial programs are available that offer a drill and practice format for instruction in basic mathematics skills. Mathematics software should be reviewed carefully before purchasing to determine whether it fulfills instructional objectives.

Reading and Writing Software

There are two types of computer software programs available for teachers of reading and writing: commercial skill-oriented instructional software and word processing programs. Each of these types of programs should be available to K-12 teachers. The skill-oriented programs are a drill and practice format which focuses upon discrete skill formation where a repetitive format is needed. Rubin states that this type of software usually focuses on a word or a sentence format.[7] Rubin also found that the majority of commercial software programs available in language arts is of the drill and practice format which is useful only in grammar, punctuation, vocabulary, and spelling. Collis and Green state that there are few commercial software programs that focus on the critical thinking skills involved in reading and writing.[8]

In language arts some drill and practice is desirable for certain instructional objectives; however, available software for teachers should be balanced with an embedded approach that combines drill and practice with a critical thinking and a problem-solving format. English and writing teachers should have both types of programs available in the classroom. If the school cannot fund enough computers and software for the English classrooms, then computers and software should be available in the library media technology center for all English teachers and their students. All students should learn to use and have access to the major word-processing programs. In language arts K-12 word processing offers teachers creativity and students relief from drill and practice. Word-processing programs can be utilized in a simplified manner or a sophisticated manner depending upon instructional objectives and level of computer competence of the teacher.

Science Software

Science teachers should be provided with several science software programs of their choice that provide meaningful scientific experiences for students. Science software should provide experiences that are attractive to learners while developing inquiry skills that are relevant to the problems of our society. Videotapes are widely used in science instruction; however, simulation software is gaining popularity. Simulation programs allow students to become part of the simulated problem while manipulating information and making creative decisions. The advantage of simulation programs rather than videotape is that the student is able to become directly involved with the interactive process of making decisions and problem solving. The ability to alter visualization is offered, and the demonstration can be repeated at student volition.

In addition, science applications software such as MBLs, data base programs, graphing programs, and spreadsheets have considerable value to help achieve instructional objectives. The computer is also valuable to the science classroom as a tool for data collection, analysis, and displays that can be manipulated as the student desires. Software programs that stress inquiry and creative thinking, a broader view of science that includes technological awareness, and a more positive attitude toward science are especially important when choosing science education software programs.

Recommendations for Software Publishers

The responsibility of software publishers is to fulfill teacher needs when designing instructional software to facilitate use in a whole class setting. In order to build confidence for the classroom teacher, publishers should develop accompanying software for all textbooks with appropriate guidelines for teacher use in a classroom setting. Instructionally effective software must meet both student and teacher needs.

Software publishers should develop software that teachers can utilize in a confident manner which addresses both repetitive activities and critical thinking skills for grade levels K-12. Instructionally effective software must meet both student and teacher needs. Software should be designed to be easily integrated into the instruction in a facile manner that mirrors teacher needs. Software must be accompanied with complete instructional strategies for use in student-centered situations, for both small groups and individualized instruction.

All textbooks and accompanying software should include teaching objectives, complete lesson plans, whole class activities, and a teacher-friendly, step-by-step manual that includes trouble-shooting of the common student errors that students may be expected to make. All instructional materials should stress relevance and appropriateness of the computer, while emphasizing instructional strategies that are most effective with the use of computers in a whole class setting. The designers and developers of commercial software should be aware of the current instructional research in each subject area at every grade level, in order to develop the most instructionally effective software possible.

Notes

1. E. O'Donnell, "Teacher Perceptions of Their Personal Computer Needs to Integrate Computers into Their Classroom Instruction" (Ed. D. diss., University of Southern California, 1991): 58-62.
2. N. Hativa, "Differential Effectiveness of Computer-Based Drill and Practice in Arithmetic" (paper presented at the annual meeting of The American Education Research Association, Washington, D.C., 1987): 3.
3. Ibid.
4. W. Bozeman and P. Burns, "Computer Assisted Instruction and Mathematics Achievement: Is There a Relationship?" *Educational Technology* 21, no. 1 (1981): 32-40.
5. N. Hativa, "Computer-Based Drill and Practice in Arithmetic: Widening the Gap between High and Low Achieving Students." *American Educational Research Journal* 25, no. 3 (1988): 366-397.
6. E. Gibb and A. Castenada, "Experiences for Young Children," in *Mathematics Learning in Early Childhood*, ed. J. Payne (Reston, VA: National Council of Teachers in Mathematics, 1975): 95-124.
7. A. Rubin, "Computer Confronts Language Arts: Cans and Shoulds for Education," in *Classroom Computers and Cognitive Science*, ed. A. C. Wilkinson (New York: Academic Press, 1983): 201-218.

8. B. Collis and V. Green, "Language Arts in Microcomputer Software for the Primary Grades: What's Available and What's It Like? Prime Areas," *Journal of the British Columbia Primary Teachers' Association* 27, no. 1 (1984): 21-24.

Chapter 13

A FRAMEWORK FOR IN-SERVICE TRAINING

The major components of planning are the same for each district; however, the specific plans and the implementation process will vary. Just as teachers of each district differ as to educational background and computer training, so will the curriculum and classroom practices of teachers differ. These guidelines allow colleges and school districts to insert their individual educational characteristics into the framework for implementation.

Strategic planning focused on specific teacher needs and predetermined goals is paramount to successful in-service. Goals should be written in an easy-to-understand form emphasizing instructional activities to implement computers in the classroom. The resulting plans, which should flow naturally from the goals, must be written to cover an ongoing period of time, preferably from six to ten years. The plans should be flexible enough to address instructional needs as they arise. The specific activities to achieve the stated goals must be clearly outlined, stated in concrete terms, then widely circulated to all who are to participate in the training.

A major goal of strategic planning is to implement computers into instruction as easily as possible with few initial classroom changes. It must be recognized that the integration of computers into the classroom is a slow, ongoing process for teachers and cannot be hurried. Teachers must fully accept computers in the classroom and have ample time to arrive at successful integration. Flexibility to move at the teachers' pace must be built into the initial strategic planning process.

Input from all teachers who are to participate in the in-service program should be solicited. The strategic plan should be delineated in a dynamic document that is capable of change when initial goals are achieved and additional goals are required. The computer integration plan should be flexible enough to encompass new advances in computer technology with a minimum of effort, and at the same time prescribe a firm foundation of training for classroom teachers. Computers must be placed in an accessible location for classroom teachers, preferably a minimum of three computers in each classroom or a desk console for teachers and laptops for students. If funding does not allow this, enough computers should be placed in the library media technology center to serve an entire class.

Computer Fund

Initial planning decisions to address are the amount of funds to allot for in-service training; placement of computers; and design, development, and implementation of the computer skills sessions to be offered to classroom teachers. The allotment of funds must be addressed in a candid manner with the knowledge that an ongoing in-service program for teachers will require a stable and consistently funded budget over a sustained period of time. Categorical funds must be alloted for hardware, software, and qualified personnel to design, develop, and implement training sessions. The establishment of a stable, consistently funded classroom computer integration fund should be agreed upon and a specific monetary amount determined and placed in the fund to be used as needed. Once the categorical computer fund is established, a concerted effort to sustain the initial fund should be encouraged.

The Computer Integration Plan

The computer integration plan must focus upon teacher needs and the strategic instructional activities that are necessary to implement computers into classroom instruction. An identification of teacher needs is the primary factor in successful staff development programs for computer integration. The plan must progress from hands-on skills to more sophisticated instructional uses of computers in the classroom in a sequential pattern based upon identified teacher needs. The scope of training should focus on the computer skills that teachers deem necessary while slowly drawing them into more sophisticated modes of computer use in the classroom.

Planning should begin with a specifically delineated document that is distributed to all interested persons. Included in this planning document should be a mission statement that is constructed in such a manner that the goals and activities for in-service naturally evolve from the mission statement.

Preparation for In-service Training

Before beginning a program of computer in-service, teachers should be prepared. In order for teachers to understand the goals of the program, a campaign of public information concerning in-service should be offered to teachers, with an opportunity to participate in all of the activities.

The plan should encompass a strong implementation model that is written in easy-to-understand terms and communicated to teachers. In addition, before beginning the program, it is important to identify which teachers are currently utilizing computers in the classroom and how the computers are being used. An identification of successful computer-using teachers will allow a pool of names from which to draw for teachers to model successful instructional computer uses in the classroom.

The acquisition of sufficient hardware and software for classrooms and the library media technology center is necessary for teachers to make the large investment of time and effort that is needed. Teachers should be assured that the hardware and the software will be there for them once they have invested their time and efforts in the computer in-service program.

Large-screen monitors for both the library media technology center and classrooms are a necessity. Development of software packages that include lesson plans and instructional strategies for each academic area utilizing the software that has been purchased is required to facilitate the integration process for teachers. All curricular changes should be framed to encompass the classroom use of computers. Software should be included with all curriculum changes.

Key Areas of Staff Development

There are three key areas of staff development that are crucial to in-service success. However, an identification of teacher needs is the primary factor in successful staff development programs for computer integration. These three areas are:

- administrative commitment and support for teachers
- teacher involvement in planning, design, and development
- teacher incentives

The level of commitment and support by the administration must be consistent, ongoing, and demonstrated by adequate funding. A respect for teacher empowerment for the acquisition of instructional strategies, merged with hands-on skills, is the key to effective in-service. In addition, administrative support must be evident at all levels from superintendent through department chairs.

Teachers must be involved throughout the entire staff development program, from the initial planning to the evaluation stage. Specific teacher needs must be targeted at all stages of the program. Teacher instructional support must be evidenced by employing an instructional design technologist as a member of the permanent full-time professional staff.

Teacher incentives must include time and funding to pursue instructional computer training. Retraining packages and release time or sabbaticals must be made available for teachers to acquire classroom computer integration skills.

The integration of computers into the classroom on a widespread basis is dependent upon the above factors. To facilitate the integration of computers into the classroom, the responsibilities of time and funding must be shifted from teachers. Teachers cannot be expected to teach, to redesign classroom activities, and to acquire and fund their own training. The progression of training should be determined by teacher readiness. In-service training for computer integration should be based upon educationally sound teaching techniques, offered at a convenient time for teachers and extending for an ongoing period of time.

In-service sessions should focus only on classroom uses of computers, not on a full range of technology. Teacher readiness should determine when more sophisticated uses of technology are introduced. Teacher needs should be specifically addressed by grade level group and by subject area. Large numbers of teachers, such as whole districts or schools, should not receive computer training simultaneously, because the instructional computer needs of teachers are different at varying grade levels.

Hands-on operational skills should be merged with student-centered classroom strategies. The focus should be on instructional strategies and teacher-directed instruction that allow teachers to begin integrating computers in the classroom immediately. Teachers' perceived needs must be identified and an in-service training program designed to focus on these needs. Progression from hands-on activities to more sophisticated uses of computers should occur as teachers are ready. In planning for computer in-service of teachers, a recognition of factors indicative of successful in-service will enhance implementation. Addressing these factors initially will enhance teacher acceptance and cooperation.

Before Beginning In-service Training

Identify the perceived computer needs of the teachers who are to participate in the in-service program and address instructional computer use specifically. Each training session should focus on the previously identified needs of the classroom teachers. Sessions should be designed that address teacher computer needs by grade level and by subject area. Initial training should begin with an emphasis on the usefulness of computers in the classroom, then progress to hands-on operational skills merged with teacher-directed, student-centered strategies.

All curriculum should be developed to facilitate the use of computers in the classroom. Specific instructional enablers for classroom teachers, such as lesson plans, appropriate instructional strategies, and classroom dynamics should be included with all curriculum developments. In-service should be designed to progress slowly and systematically based on teacher readiness for more interactive and sophisticated uses of computers. Teachers should have frequent opportunities to practice their newly-learned skills as they progress to each level of computer use. A program of district-wide and on-site recognition should be established for teachers who are integrating computers into the classroom.

A degreed, certificated instructional design technologist should be employed at the district level to develop in-service sessions and to work collaboratively with the local college of education. A certificated library media technology teacher should be employed at each school site to assist teachers with integration of computers in the classroom.

An active ongoing public relations program should be established to inform teachers of the goals and objectives of the computer integration in-service program. An ongoing relationship with local newspapers, radio, and television stations to spotlight exemplary instructional computer innovations will encourage teachers to sustain their efforts to integrate computers into classroom instruction.

Factors of Successful In-Service Training

Successful in-service training will include incentives for participating teachers. Teacher incentives should include frequent opportunities to share successful computer applications with colleagues and to observe colleagues modeling successful computer instructional strategies. Also important are release days with funds supplied to attend professional computer conferences and networking sessions.

Convenient access to appropriate curriculum-related software designed with teacher-directed and student-intensive instructional strategies that utilize computers in a whole class environment is primary to successful computer integration. Software must be merged with the curriculum and fulfill a curricular objective as textbooks do. All software for classroom teachers should be accompanied by an instructional use package which includes instructional strategies for small-group student-centered activities and whole class instructional strategies.

Recognition that in-service training is an ongoing experience and a process of changing instructional methods is of primary importance for successful in-service training. Teachers must learn a new way of teaching. This is a personal experience for teachers that requires time and effort, therefore, ongoing sustained support for all classroom teachers is essential for the duration of the computer integration process.

Computer integration efforts must encompass a firm foundation of basic skills to enable teachers to begin utilizing computers in classroom instruction immediately. A focus specifically on the instructional uses of computers and an emphasis on teacher-directed and student-specific utilization of computers is mandatory. Various instructional uses of computers in the classroom, such as computer assisted instruction, computer managed instruction, tutorials, drill and practice, simulations, and authoring packages, should be stressed. Each teacher should understand the appropriate uses of computers in differing instructional situations, and when to employ each. Teachers should be encouraged to become familiar with appropriate software for their subject area. Textbooks that have accompanying software and instructional use packages should be supplied.

Successful computer integration should necessitate as few changes as possible for classroom teachers. Teachers must have time to adapt and to incorporate the changes that are necessary. As teachers grow confident with their computer skills they become empowered to integrate computers into classroom instruction. Teacher empowerment should offer the knowledge necessary to expand instructional computer skills and to become successful users of computers in the classroom.

Constraints to Successful Computer Integration

The most common constraint to successful computer integration is a lack of whole class teaching strategies to employ with computers. Other common constraints are the lack of basic hands-on computer skills, the location of computers in relation to the classroom, teachers who are overburdened with curricular and extra-curricular duties, a lack of teacher incentives to utilize computers in the classroom, and a lack of teacher support while learning to utilize computers in the classroom. Also restrictive to successful instructional computer use are teacher perceptions regarding the instructional use of computers in the classroom and the current instructional use of computers as they correspond with the organizational patterns of the school. It is impossible for teachers to change class schedules and closed classrooms without administrative approval.

Computer integration into instruction can be accomplished with a single computer in the classroom if teachers have access to full class computers in the library media technology center so that individual students may have hands-on experience simultaneously. Basic level competencies should be addressed in all training sessions. Progress to more sophisticated classroom computer applications, such as interactive video/computer, laser discs, net-working, information highway, and electronic searching, only as teachers demonstrate that they are ready for more advanced uses.

Hands-on activities, including keyboarding, basic operations of computers, troubleshooting, and learning the capabilities of different brands, should be offered at the appropriate level of teacher expertise. Instructional uses of software including an explanation of the different types of software, i.e., drill and practice, tutorials, simulations, CAI, CMI, branching programs, games, CD-ROM, and hypercard should be offered throughout the in-service program.

A familiarity with the different types of software and a variety of whole class instructional strategies is primary to the instructional use of computers. In addition, practices which protect hardware and software and copyright and fair use practices should be offered to teachers. Ongoing instruction in hardware and software use should be offered in the classroom for the convenience of the teacher. Also, the time to practice new skills should be readily available for teachers.

A network of variables, each influencing the other and all influencing the teacher, interact to control, to facilitate, or to act as barriers to the integration of computers into the classroom. A successful in-service plan will address these barriers and the influences they exert on teachers. The unique constraints to the integration of computers into the classroom should be identified before the computer integration plan is written. The constraints to instructional computer use will vary with each district; however, some of the most common constraints have been listed above.

Computer in-service should be based upon the philosophy that teachers wish to integrate computers into their classrooms, that teachers' computer needs differ at different grade levels and with different subject areas, and that teachers wish to receive teacher-directed student-centered strategies appropriate for a whole class setting. Also, successful computer training should bring a minimum of change with no coercion or sudden unexpected changes for teachers.

Summary

The emphasis of all in-service sessions should be on teacher-identified needs and ease of use. Teacher-directed whole class instructional strategies will facilitate the integration of computers for teachers. Each in-service session should acquaint teachers with the software that is to be used in the classroom. In addition, teachers should be introduced to the appropriate instructional strategies to utilize with the software. Accompanying instructional packages should be included with all software. Teachers should also be told how and where to obtain the software and accompanying instructional package.

The software packages should include complete lesson plans, student-centered activities, and teacher directed strategies appropriate for a whole class setting. These instructional strategies should be designed to move teachers from traditional teaching methods to new technologies, such as electronic blackboards, large-screen monitors, electronic pens, and interactive hardware.

Sustaining personnel should be available on demand for teachers to guide them with newly formed computer skills as they learn to use computers as an instructional tool. Teachers should understand that the freedom to change classsroom dynamics and make innovative classroom changes as they progress to full classroom computer integration is supported by the administration.

Chapter 14

A CALL FOR NATIONAL COMPUTER STANDARDS FOR TEACHER TRAINING

Dyrli and Kinnaman state that making the transition from the classroom of the past to the classroom of the future requires a fundamental departure from current practice. They also state that making the transformation successfully requires a basic understanding of the fundamental difference between education in the industrial age and education in the information age and the logical steps of how to change today's schools into the ones needed for tomorrow.[1] The purpose of this book is to offer school administrators and classroom teachers the knowledge they need to begin making this transition.

The philosophy that drives today's educational process must significantly change if computer integration is to be achieved. This book has identified some of the significant areas in which change must become apparent. The basic structure of the process of in-service for the integration of computers into the classroom must be changed. When teachers become confident with the computer skills and instructional strategies that are necessary to integrate computers into the classroom, the educational process will adapt to the new beliefs and pedagogical methods.

Schools will not be changed without the cooperation of the classroom teacher. However, the classroom teacher is not able to change traditional classroom practice without the necessary skills. In 1994, the California Media and Library Educators Association surveyed more than 200 members concerning technology use in California schools. The results of this survey showed that the number one concern among members was how to create and use lessons that integrate computers into the classroom.[2] Considering that school library media technology teachers work closely with classroom teachers, this survey confirms the research of O'Donnell, who found that classroom teachers wish to integate computers into classrooms, but do not know how.[3]

Teachers have voiced a desire to acquire the instructional strategies that lead from traditional methods of instruction to more modern methods. However, preservice and in-service education does not offer these skills to teachers. It is impossible to take advantage of the benefits that computers in the classroom offer without knowledgeable and computer-literate teachers. Fullan believes that educators must respond to teacher desires if computers are to become a viable component of the classroom.[4]

This is a circular problem. To enjoy an information age classroom teachers must become proactive, but before they can be proactive, they must realize the full potential of computers integrated into the curriculum. Teachers must move from traditional classroom methods to the instructional methods that utilize computers. If teachers do not know how to do this, it will remain a circular problem of inaction.

When colleges of education and school districts offer teachers the training that is necessary to integate computers into the classroom, computers will be integrated on a widespread basis. Teachers must become confident and comfortable working in an information age classroom. Without knowledge of teacher-directed classroom strategies, classrooms will remain the traditional setting they are today. State and national guidelines must include measures to encourage the use of classroom computers.

As funding is alloted for hardware and software, teacher training at both the preservice and the in-service levels must be part of the funding package. There must be a concerted effort at all levels to train teachers appropriately for the integration of computers into the classroom. The recognition that teachers are the key to widespread integration of computers into the classroom equates with a successful transition to the electronic classroom of tomorrow.

A Call for National Standards for Computer Education

In this proposed climate of cooperation between school districts and colleges of education, national standards based upon reliable research should be developed to offer institutions responsible for training teachers specific guidelines by which to design and develop teacher training and education to integrate computers in the classroom. Some states have developed standards and taken action to determine whether teachers have met the standards. However, the standards that have been developed address only the basics of computer skills and do not address the necessary computer education that teachers need to integrate computers into the classroom. The majority of teachers receive virtually no training in the student-centered classroom strategies that merge the use of computers with instruction. Computer integration is still in the trial and error period, without guidelines for school districts to follow when developing master plans. In-service programs for computer use should be guided by standards that offer teachers the classroom-centered instructional skills that they need.

National Teacher In-service Instructional Computer Standards

Following are recommendations for national computer standards for teachers to enable the integration of computers into classrooms in a reasonable length of time and in a successful and cost-effective manner. There are three primary areas that should be addressed. Each of these areas will fulfill a foundational need for classroom teachers.

The first area is a change in teachers' beliefs concerning computers. Teachers must realize the efficacy of computers in the classroom. The second area deals with basic computer skills. Hands-on skills and instructional strategies must be combined if successful computer integration programs are to be developed. The third area deals with the instructional skills that teachers need in order to integrate computers into classrooms. Training programs must empower teachers for computer use in instruction. Teachers cannot utilize computers effectively in the classroom without primary computer skills merged with instructional strategies appropriate for a whole class setting.

In-service training sessions must acquaint teachers with the usefulness of computers in the classroom. Teachers should be shown exemplary instructional uses as they are taught hands-on skills and keyboarding. Basic to the utilization of computers in the classroom is a knowledge of how to use different software programs and understand copyrights. Very important to classroom computer use is an understanding of how to connect video monitor, laser disc hardware, computer, and printer, how to correct common student errors, and how to rearrange the classroom effectively for student computer use.

Teachers have expressed a desire to utilize computers in a whole class setting. In order to do this effectively, teachers must understand the specific teaching strategies to employ with computers in a whole class setting with small-group cooperative learning, paired cooperative use of computers, and individual learners utilizing computers independently. Inherent in the whole class utilization of computers is an understanding of the appropriate instructional strategies to employ in each learning situation and with the instructional software.

Teachers also must understand the best fit for software with specific lessons, the appropriate teaching strategies to employ with each type of software, and the most effective teaching methods to use with each lesson utilizing computers. An understanding of which lessons can be improved and enhanced by computers is primary to the effective integration of computers in the classroom.

As teachers learn which instructional strategies to employ with the classroom utilization of computers they will wish to progress to more sophisticated uses of computers, such as how to incorporate interactive computer/video in instruction, how to utilize the information highway and other on-line technologies, how to conduct electronic searching, and how best to combine print sources with electronic searching.

A primary source of assistance for classroom teachers as they learn to merge computers with their instruction is the school library technology teacher. The school librarian has a knowledge of the resources, pedagogical techniques, and appropriate technology. This professional is on-site to offer sustained assistance when needed by teachers. The progress of computer integration in the classroom has been slow because of a lack of funds to support the appropriate sustained computer training that teachers require to feel confident of their ability to utilize computers successfully in their classrooms.

National Teacher Training Programs for Computer Education

The federal government has played a traditional role in providing national leadership in education. Currently, there are many federal sources for funding that support teacher training. However, these sources of funds are located within various agencies. These agencies of funding should be combined into one department that would be responsible for the funding of training or the retraining of teachers for instructional computer use. The federal government should also encourage cooperation between school districts and colleges of education with the formation of national computer standards and the appropriation of adequate funding for effective computer training of teachers.

On April 18, 1991, then-President Bush announced America 2000: An Education Strategy. This plan will move America toward national education goals. As part of America 2000, standards for education are being developed in conjunction with the National Education Goals panel. In January 1993, Education Secretary Riley stated four objectives that would guide him as Education Secretary.[5] These goals are to improve the quality of education, to assure access and opportunity for students, to foster cooperation between schools and colleges, and to help all students achieve the high standards stated in the America 2000 goals.[5]

These standards represent what students will need to know to function in today's world and in the twenty-first century. A focus is also needed on the skills that teachers require to help students progress into the information-age classroom. Students do not achieve without guidance and assistance. If education is to move forward, teachers must have access to the education that will help them guide the students of tomorrow. Teachers must acquire the instructional computer skills that are needed to integrate computers into the classroom on a widespread basis in an effective manner.

This book proposes that not only should standards for students' education but also standards for teachers' instructional computer education should be developed. The standards for teacher training must address the specific needs of teachers to integrate computers in the classroom. There must be specific guidelines based on reliable research findings framed for the instructional computer education of teachers. The standards should include technical knowledge of computers, teacher-dircted pedagogical methods utilizing computers, and the classroom student-centered instructional strategies which are necessary to integrate computers into classrooms.

The America 2000 education goals should also include funding distributed directly to teachers for a training or a retraining package. *America 2000: An Education Strategy* states that education is not free, but ingenuity, commitment, and accountability matter more than money.[6] The funds required to train or to retrain dedicated teachers with an innovative commitment to computers in the classroom would be minimal compared to the duplication of effort and expense that is currently the norm.

The Goals 2000 Act will provide support for each state and school district to develop a comprehensive action plan to restructure schools. The Education Improvement Act of 1994 provided $393 million in fiscal year 1994 to assist states in planning reforms and putting them in place. Future reforms should include funding for strategic restructuring of teacher training programs for the integration of computers into the classroom throughout all educational levels.

Computers have been in schools for twenty years. However, little progress has been made in the integration of computers in the classroom. Teachers must have the skills to effectively organize and conduct projects in an electronic classroom. As we enter the information age, it is time to ensure all teachers access to the computer skills and instructional knowledge they need to function in a global classroom with an address on the electronic information super-highway.

Notes

1. O. Dryli and D. Kinnaman, "Preparing for the Integration of Emerging Technologies," *Technology and Learning* 14, no. 8 (1994): 92.
2. California Media and Library Educators Association, "Educational Technology Survey," *CMLEA Newsletter* 18, no. 3 (1994): 3.
3. E. O'Donnell, "Teacher Perceptions of Their Personal Computer Needs to Integrate Computers Into Their Classroom Instruction." (Ed. D. diss., University of Southern California, 1991).
4. M. Fullan, *The Meaning of Educational Change* (New York, Teachers College Press, 1982): 53-55.
5. R. Riley, *Goals 2000, Educate America: Community Update* (U. S. Department of Education, Washington, DC, no. 1, 1993)
6. Ibid.

Appendix A

SURVEY QUESTIONNAIRE

SCANTRON INSTRUCTIONS: Please mark with a #2 pencil on the accompanying Scantron sheet.

Part I.   General Information

   1.   In what area of education do you work?
         (a)   Classroom teacher
         (b)   Resource teacher K - 6
         (c)   Resource teacher 6 - 8
         (d)   Special Ed
         (e)   District specialist

   2.   What grade level(s) do you teach or what are your responsibility levels?
         (a)   K - 3
         (b)   4 - 6
         (c)   7 - 8
         (d)   9 - 12
         (e)   All

   3.   Do you own a personal computer?
         (a)   Yes
         (b)   No

   4.   If yes, what type?
         (a)   Macintosh
         (b)   Apple
         (c)   IBM/IBM compatible
         (d)   TRS
         (e)   Other

   5.   Do you use a computer at your school site?
         (a)   Yes
         (b)   No

6.   Do you use videos at your school site?
     (a)   Yes
     (b)   No

Part II.   Computer Training

7.   At what level do you consider your skills
     regarding computer operation?
     (a)   Beginner
     (b)   Intermediate user
     (c)   Advanced user

In which areas would you participate in training to improve <u>your</u>
<u>personal</u> computer skills to utilize computers in classroom instruction?
MARK (a) Yes or (b) No on Numbers 8 - 13.

8.   Intro to computer use
     (a)   Yes
     (b)   No

9.   Word processing
     (a)   Yes
     (b)   No

10. Data base
     (a)   Yes
     (b)   No

11. Spread sheets
     (a)   Yes
     (b)   No

12. Graphics
     (a)   Yes
     (b)   No

13. Desktop publishing
     (a)   Yes
     (b)   No

In which of the following <u>strategies</u> would you like additional training? MARK (a) Yes or (b) No on Numbers 14 - 20.

14. Using software for individualized instruction
    (a) Yes
    (b) No

15. Using software for small group cooperative learning activities
    (a) Yes
    (b) No

16. Using software for teacher-directed lessons
    (a) Yes
    (b) No

17. Developing print support materials
    (a) Yes
    (b) No

18. Teaching students about computers
    (a) Yes
    (b) No

19. Editing or authoring computer software for student use
    (a) Yes
    (b) No

20. Procedures for evaluating instructional software
    (a) Yes
    (b) No

Part III. Computer Use

21. How many computers do you have in your classroom?
    (a) 0
    (b) 1
    (c) 2 - 5

         (d)   6 - 10
         (e)   over 10

In which of the following situations are your students currently using computers in their instruction? MARK (a) Yes or (b) No on Numbers 22 - 28.

    22.   Your classroom
         (a)   Yes
         (b)   No

    23.   Another classroom
         (a)   Yes
         (b)   No

    24.   Computer Lab
         (a)   Yes
         (b)   No

    25.   Library Media Center
         (a)   Yes
         (b)   No

    26.   Resource Center
         (a)   Yes
         (b)   No

    27.   Portable Computer
         (a)   Yes
         (b)   No

    28.   None of the above
         (a)   Yes
         (b)   No

What type of computers are you using for your classroom/computer lab? MARK (a) Yes or (b) No on Numbers 29 - 32.

    29.   Macintosh
         (a)   Yes

    (b) No

30. Apple
    (a) Yes
    (b) No

31. TRS
    (a) Yes
    (b) No

32. IBM/IBM compatible
    (a) Yes
    (b) No

33. On a weekly basis, how much time (on the
    average) do your students spend on computers in
    the classroom or computer lab?
    (a) 0
    (b) 15 - 29 min.
    (c) 30 - 59 min.
    (d) 1 - 4 hours
    (e) 5 or more hours

34. How many hours weekly do <u>you</u> use computers in
    <u>direct</u> classroom instruction?
    (a) 0
    (b) 15 - 29 min.
    (c) 30 - 59 min.
    (d) 1 - 4 hours
    (e) 5 or more hours

Do you use computers in any of the following ways? MARK (a) Yes
or (b) No for Numbers 35 - 39.

35. To introduce a lesson
    (a) Yes
    (b) No

36. Follow-up to a lesson
    (a) Yes

(b)   No

37.   To supplement lessons
       (a)   Yes
       (b)   No

38.   To reinforce lessons
       (a)   Yes
       (b)   No

39.   To teach about computers
       (a)   Yes
       (b)   No

In which of the following areas do you use computers to support instruction? MARK (a) Yes or (b) No for Numbers 40 - 52.

40.   Mathematics
       (a)   Yes
       (b)   No

41.   Writing
       (a)   Yes
       (b)   No

42.   Foreign language
       (a)   Yes
       (b)   No

43.   Reading
       (a)   Yes
       (b)   No

44.   Science/Health
       (a)   Yes
       (b)   No

45.   Business Education
       (a)   Yes
       (b)   No

46. Art
    (a) Yes
    (b) No

47. English/Language
    (a) Yes
    (b) No

48. Social Studies
    (a) Yes
    (b) No

49. Music
    (a) Yes
    (b) No

50. Physical Education
    (a) Yes
    (b) No

51. ESL
    (a) Yes
    (b) No

52. Bilingual Education
    (a) Yes
    (b) No

Appendix B

RESULTS

The purpose of this study was to assess the teachers' self-perceived needs for further computer training and their self-perceived level of computer skills and to determine in which computer strategies teachers would like to receive further training. Descriptive statistics for each of the nine research questions are reported, and each research question is answered through interpretation of the data.

In order to provide the reader with a clear understanding of the results of this study, the data analysis is reported by research question. Each research question has its own subheading and contains the data for a survey question used to answer that particular research question. Appropriate tables are provided to facilitate comprehension of the data.

The first subsection, Data Analysis, is a brief summary description of the sampling procedure. Each subsection that follows pertains to a research question. Contained in each subsection is the survey data, which answer each question, followed by the descriptive data in table form.

An alpha level of .05 was used for deciding statistical significance for all measures of association (chi-square). The total number of teachers who participated in the study was 728, of which 16 were resource teachers, 89 were special education teachers, 16 were English as a second language teachers, and 623 were regular classroom teachers. When the data concerns all the teachers who participated in the study, $N=728$; when data concern the grade levels K-12, $N=628$. When $N=623$ is used, resource teachers and the special education teachers are not included.

Another reason why the sample size differs occasionally is because it is likely that some of the teachers answered questions 1 and 2 of the survey independently. For example, on Question 2, some resource teachers and special education teachers (as has been indicated in Question 1) also classified themselves as classroom teachers on question 2. In that instance, it was necessary to use the total number, $N=728$, as the classroom teacher information for Question 2. In addition, all of the teachers did not answer all of the questions. This was taken into consideration when responses were tabulated.

Data Analysis

As noted above, the final return rate was 728 surveys, for a return rate of 85 percent. The survey answer sheets were tabulated by the district data processing center. The total number of responses for each question on the survey was totaled, the means and percentages were calculated, and the number of responses in each category were then totaled. Research Questions 1, 2, 8, and 9 were analyzed using frequency distributions and percentages only. Research Questions 5 and 6, which utilize multiple responses, were analyzed using contingency analyses of cell frequency and percentages. Research Questions 3, 4, 5, 6, and 7 were analyzed using contingency analyses and chi-square statistics. It may be important to note that only 2-3 percent difference was apparent for some of the response totals.

Question 1.

In which computer strategies do teachers wish more computer training?

Questions 14 through 20 were used to answer this research Question. The data for Questions 14-20 are shown in Table 1 and are arranged from high to low by the total number of Yes answers.

The majority of teachers (71.96%) desired to receive training in utilizing software for small-group cooperative learning. Using software for individualized instruction was the second most important computer strategy for the teachers, with 70.03 percent responding that they would like to receive training in this strategy.

Procedures for evaluating instructional software was the least important strategy for teachers (38.05%). Editing and authoring computer software for student use was also one of the least preferred strategies, with 38.95 percent of the teachers responding that they would like to receive training in this strategy.

Table 1. Responses to Survey Questions 14-20 Regarding Teacher Preferences for Computer Training Strategies.

(*N*=728)

Ques. No.	Desires training in which computer strategy	Yes		No		Total	
		N	%	*N*	%	*N*	%
15	Using software for small group cooperative learning	503	71.96	196	28.04	699	100
14	Using software for indvidualized learning	491	70.03	210	29.97	701	100
16	Using software for teacher-directed lessons	459	65.94	237	65.94	696	100
17	Developing print support materials	437	62.97	257	37.03	694	100
18	Teaching students about computers	341	48.99	355	51.01	696	100
19	Editing/Authoring computer software for student use	271	38.95	425	61.05	696	100
20	Evaluating instructional software	266	38.05	433	61.95	699	100

Question 2

In which subject areas do teachers use computers the greatest percentage of the time to support instruction?

Questions 40-52 were used to answer this research question. The data for Questions 40-54 are listed in Table 2 and are arranged from high to low by the total number of Yes answers.

The largest percentage of teachers (36.05%) utilize computers in mathematics instruction. The next subject area where computers were most utilized in instruction was writing (32.95%). Computers were utilized least in music (2.11%). Physical education was the next least (3.00%) subject area in which computers were utilized in instruction.

Table 2. Responses to Survey Questions 40-52 Regarding Which Areas Teachers Use Computers to Support Instruction.

(N=728)

Ques.	Computer Use in Instruction	Yes		No		Total	
		N	%	N	%	N	%
40	Mathematics	247	36.05	438	63.95	685	100
41	Writing	229	32.95	466	67.05	695	100
43	Reading	228	32.95	464	67.05	692	100
47	English Language	204	30.01	475	69.99	679	100
48	Social Studies	95	13.98	585	86.02	680	100
51	English as a second language	76	10.99	616	89.01	692	100
44	Science/ Health	60	8.73	627	91.27	687	100
46	Art	47	6.95	629	93.85	676	100
52	Bilingual Education	48	6.96	642	93.04	690	100
42	Foreign Language	28	4.05	664	95.95	692	100
50	Physical Education	20	3.00	654	97.00	754	100
49	Music	14	2.11	649	97.87	663	100

Question 3

At which levels of education (K-3, 4-6, 7-8, 9-12) do students use computers the greatest percentage of time?

The percentages are reported for four grade level groupings and four time frames. Question 33 was used to answer this research question. The data are listed in Table 3 and are organized by time and reported by grade levels. The data are reported by percentage of time that students spend using computers in classroom instruction per week.

The chi-square analysis yielded a chi-square value of 70.14 with $p = 00$. This finding indicates that there is a significant relationship between time and grade level. Teachers of grades 7-12 were more likely to answer none, while the lower grade teachers (K-3) were more likely to answer 15-29 minutes.

As noted in Table 3, K-3 students utilize computers between 15-29 minutes in classroom instruction, whereas grades 7-8 and 9-12 students are less likely to use computers in their classroom instruction. Thus, students in levels K-3 are spending more time on computers than students in grades 4-6, 7-8, or 9-12.

Table 3. Time Per Week (in Minutes) Students Spend on Computers in the Classroom.

Grade Level	Time				Total
	None	15-29	30-59	60+	*N*
K-3					
N	60	80	44	16	200
%	30.00	40.00	22.00	8.00	100
4-6					
N	32	45	39	18	134
%	23.88	33.58	29.10	13.43	100
7-8					
N	63	23	13	15	114
%	55.26	20.18	11.40	13.16	100
9-12					
N	120	56	20	29	22
%	53.33	24.89	8.89	12.89	100

Note: χ^2 (9, $N = 673$) = 70.41, $p = .00$.

Question 4

On a weekly basis, which teachers (classroom teachers, resource teachers, and special education teachers) spend the greatest percentage of time utilizing computers in direct classroom instruction?

The data from Question 34 are used to answer this research question. The data are presented in Table 4 by hours and minutes on a weekly basis and are organized by time reported by type of teacher (classroom, resource, and special education). The data are also reported by percentage of time that the teachers spend utilizing computers in direct classroom instruction for one week.

There were no significant findings. One third of the cells have expected counts of less than five. Therefore, a chi-square analysis may not be a valid test. However, a chi-square analysis was performed which yielded a chi-square value of 9.841 with $p = .13$. It is also important to note that the table output is greater than sample size, indicating that some of the teachers answered Questions, 1 and 2 of the survey independently, in that on Question 2, some of the resource and special education teachers also classified themselves as classroom teachers.

The results indicated that 72.89 percent of classroom teachers do not use the computer in their classroom instruction, while 7.87 percent use the computer in the instructional process for more than one hour per week. Of the resource teachers, 25 percent use computers in their instruction for more than one hour, while 62.50 percent do not use the computer in instruction. Finally, 20.31 percent of the special education teachers use computers in their instruction and 4.69 percent do not use computers in their instructional process.

Table 4. How Much Time Per Week Classroom, Resource, and Special Education Teachers Spend Utilizing Computers in Direct Classroom Instruction.

Type of Teacher	Time (minutes)				Total
	0	15-29	30-59	60+	
Classroom					
N	500	106	26	54	686
%	72.89	15.45	3.37	7.87	100
Resource					
N	10	1	1	4	16
%	62.50	6.25	6.25	25.00	100
Special Education					
N	47	13	1	3	64
%	73.44	20.31	1.56	4.69	100

Note: χ^2 (6, N= 766) = 9.841, p = .13.

Question 5

   At which grade levels do the greatest percentage of teachers
wish to receive more computer training?

   Survey Questions 8-13 were used to answer this question. The
teachers' answers were totaled and percentages were computed. The
percentages are reported by grade levels and by area of computer skill
in which the teacher wishes to receive more training. The data are
listed in Tables 5-10 and are organized by the number of the survey
question and the grade level of the respondents. Table 11, a summary
table, is included as a response summary for Questions 8-13. The
percentages which appear in the total column indicate the summary of
the percentage of "Yes" answers for grades K-12. This summary
represents the percentage of teachers, grades K-12, that desire training
in each computer skill.

Survey Question 8:   Introduction to Computers

The results to Question 8 are presented in Table 5. Of the 201 total responses, 64.18 percent of K-3 teachers would like to receive training in introduction to computers. Teachers of grades 4-6 were evenly distributed between "Yes" and "No" responses to receiving training in basic computer skills. Of the 117 responses at the 7-8 grade level, 55.56 percent of the teachers would like to receive basic computer training; of the 223 total responses at the 9-12 grade level, 52.02 percent of the teachers would like to receive such training. These differences yielded a chi-square value of 9.19, with $p = .27$.

Table 5. Which Teachers Would Participate in Training to Improve Personal Computer Skills in Introduction to Computer Use

Grade Level	Yes	No	Total
K-3			
N	129	72	201
%	64.18	35.82	100
4-6			
N	80	80	160
%	50.00	50.00	100
7-8			
N	65	52	117
%	55.56	44.44	100
9-12			
N	116	107	223
%	52.02	47.98	100

Note: χ^2 (3, $N = 701$) = 9.19, $p = .27$.

Survey Question 9:   Word Processing

The results to Question 9 are presented in Table 6. Of the 201 responses, 66.17 percent of grades K-3 teachers would like to receive training in word processing, while 67.12 percent of 4-6 grade teachers would like to receive such training. Of the 223 teachers who answered this question, 69.96 percent of the 9-12 grade teachers would like to receive training in word processing. These differences yielded a chi-square value of 12.01, with $p = .01$.

Table 6. Which Teachers Would Participate in Training to Improve Personal Computer Skills in Word Processing?

Grade Level	Yes	No	Total
K-3			
N	133	68	201
%	66.17	33.83	100
4-6			
N	98	48	146
%	67.12	32.88	100
7-8			
N	61	57	118
%	51.69	48.31	100
9-12			
N	156	67	223
%	69.96	30.04	100

Note: χ^2 (3, N = 688) = 12.01, p = .01.

Survey Question 10: Data Base Management

The results to Question 10 are presented in Table 7. Of the 198 teachers who answered this question, 48.48 percent of the grade K-3 teachers would like to receive training in data base management, and 56.66 percent of grades 4-6 teachers would like to receive training in data base management. Of the 118 grade 7-8 teachers, half answered "Yes" and half answered "No" to receiving additional computer training in data base management. Of the 223 teachers at the 9-12 grade level who answered this question, 69.96 percent would like to receive training in data base management. These differences yielded a chi-square value of 31.38, with $p = .00$.

Table 7. Which Teachers Would Participate in Training to Improve Personal Computer Skills in Data Base Management?

Grade Level	Yes	No	Total
K-3			
N	96	102	198
%	48.48	51.52	100
4-6			
N	82	63	145
%	56.55	43.45	100
7-8			
N	59	59	118
%	50.00	50.00	100
9-12			
N	163	60	223
%	73.09	26.91	100

Note: $\chi^2 (3, N = 684) = 31.48, p = .00$.

Survey Question 11:   Spreadsheets

The results to Question 11 are presented in Table 8.   At the K-3 level, 39.80 percent of teachers wish to receive training to use spreadsheets in their instruction.   Of the 146 teachers in grades 4-6, 47.26 percent would like to receive training in spreadsheets, while 223 teachers (68.16 percent) would not like to receive training in spreadsheets.   These differences yielded a chi-square value of 37.78, with $p = .00$.

Table 8. Which Teachers Would Participate in Training to Improve Personal Computer Skills in Spreadsheets?

Grade Level	Yes	No	Total
K-3			
N	80	121	201
%	39.80	60.20	100
4-6			
N	69	77	146
%	47.26	52.74	100
7-8			
N	56	63	119
%	47.06	52.94	100
9-12			
N	153	71	223
%	68.12	31.84	100

Note: χ^2 $(3, N = 689) = 37.81$, $p = .00$.

Survey Question 12: Graphics

The results to Question 12 are presented in Table 9. In grades K-3, 59.20 percent of the teachers would like to receive training in graphics, while 40.80 percent of teachers do not. Of the teachers at the 4-6 grade level, 71.92 percent would like to receive training in graphics. In grades 7-8, 61.86 percent of the 118 teachers would like to receive training in graphics. At the 9-12 grade level, of the 223 teachers who responded, 78.92 percent would like to receive training in graphics. These differences yielded a chi-square value of 22.23, with $p = .00$.

Table 9. **Which Teachers Would Participate in Training to Improve Personal Computer Skills in Graphics?**

Grade Level	Yes	No	Total
K-3			
N	119	82	201
%	59.20	40.80	100
4-6			
N	105	41	146
%	71.92	28.08	100
7-8			
N	73	45	118
%	61.86	38.14	100
9-12			
N	176	47	223
%	78.92	21.08	100

Note: χ^2 $(3, N = 688) = 22.56, p = .00$.

Survey Question 13: Desktop Publishing

The results to Question 13 are presented in Table 10. In grades K-3, 201 teachers answered this question, of which 57.21 percent would like to receive training in desktop publishing, while 42.79 percent do not wish to receive such training. At the 4-6 grade level, 146 teachers responded, 73.29 percent of whom would like to receive training in desktop publishing. At the 7-8 grade level, 124 teachers responded, 58.87 percent of whom would also like to receive such training, while 41.13 percent do not wish to receive such training. At the 9-12 grade level, 250 teachers responded to this question, of which 70.40 percent would like to receive training in desktop publishing. These differences yielded a chi-square value of 15.05, with $p = .00$.

Table 10. Which Teachers Would Participate in Training to Improve Personal Computer Skills in Desktop Publishing?

Grade Level	Yes	No	Total
K-3			
N	115	86	201
%	57.21	42.79	100
4-6			
N	107	39	146
%	73.29	26.71	100
7-8			
N	73	51	124
%	58.87	41.13	100
9-12			
N	176	74	250
%	70.40	29.60	100

Note: χ^2 (3, $N = 721$) = 15.52, $p = .00$.

Table 11. Summary of Teacher Responses Regarding Areas of Computer Use in Which They Would Like to Receive Training.

Question no. and area of computer use	Grade Level									
	K-3		4-6		7-8		9-12		Total	
	N	%	*N*	%	*N*	%	*N*	%	*N*	%
8. Basic computer skills	129	64	80	55	65	55	116	52	390	56.7
9. Word proc.	133	66	98	67	61	52	156	70	448	6.51
10. Data base	96	48	82	56	59	50	163	73	400	58.1
11. Spread sheets	80	40	69	47	56	47	152	68	357	51.9
12. Graphics	119	59	105	72	73	62	176	79	473	68.8
13. Desk top pub.	115	57	107	73	67	57	149	67	438	65.6

Note: Percentages are for "Yes" answers.

Question 6

At which grade levels do the greatest percentage of teachers wish to improve their computer strategies in using software?

Survey Questions 14-20 were used to answer this question. The teachers' answers were tabulated and percentages calculated. The percentages are reported by the computer strategy in which the teacher wishes to receive more training. The results are listed in Tables 12-18 and are reported by the greatest percentage of teachers who would like to receive training in that particular strategy at each grade level. A summary of Question 6 is provided in Table 19 (response for Questions 14-20).

Only the results to Questions 15, 17, and 18 were significant. For Question 15, the analysis yielded a chi-square value of 9.00, with $p = .03$. Of the total 102 responses for grades K-3 teachers, 75.12 percent would like to receive training in using software for small-group cooperative learning activities. At grade level 4-6, 73.97 percent of teachers would like to receive additional training in that strategy, and at grade level 9-12, 70.85 percent of the teachers who responded also would like to receive additional training in using software for small-group cooperative learning activities.

For Question 17, the analysis yielded a chi-square value of 11.16, with $p = .01$. Teachers in grades K-8 did not express as much of a desire (56.22% - 62.71%) for more training to develop print materials as did teachers at the 9-12 grade level. Of the 223 teachers responding at the 9-12 level, 70.87 percent wished to receive more training in strategies to develop computer print materials for their classroom.

For Question 18, the analysis yielded a chi-square value of 6.16, with $p = .10$. Of teachers expressing a desire to receive training in teaching students about computers, at the grade K-3 level, 60.20 percent of the teachers wished to receive more training, and at the grades 4-6 level, 54.79 percent wished to receive such training.

At the grade 7-8 and grade 9-12 levels, a greater percentage of teachers did not wish to receive additional training in teaching students about computers compared to the grade K-3 and grade 4-6 levels. Of these teachers, at grades 7-8, 60.17 percent did not desire training in this area and at grades 9-12, 65.92 percent did not desire such training.

Table 19 provides a summary of responses for Questions 14-20. The percentages that appear in the total column indicate the summary of the percentages of "Yes" answers for grades K-12. This summary represents the percentages of grade K-12 teachers who desire training in each computer skill.

Survey Question 14: Individualized Instruction

The results to Question 14 are presented in Table 12; 201 grade K-3 teachers answered this question, of which 67.16 percent responded that they would like training in using software for individualized instruction, and 66 teachers (32.84%) would not like to receive training in this strategy. At the grade 4-6 level, 146 teachers an-swered this question, and 69.86 percent of them would like to receive training in using software for individualized instruction. At the 7-8 grade level, 118 teachers responded to this question; 61.02 percent would like to receive training in using software for individualized instruction. These differences yielded a chi-square value of 3.26, with $p = .35$.

Table 12. Teachers Wishing to Improve Their Computer Strategies in Using Software for Individualized Instruction.

Grade Level	Yes	No	Total
K-3			
N	135	66	201
%	67.16	32.84	100
4-6			
N	102	44	146
%	69.86	30.14	100
7-8			
N	72	46	118
%	61.02	38.98	100
9-12			
N	156	67	223
%	69.96	30.04	100

Note: $\chi^2 (3, N = 688) = 3.26$, $p = .35$.

Survey Question 15: Using Software for Small-Group Cooperative Learning

The results to Question 15 are presented in Table 12. Of the 201 teachers of grades K-3 who responded to this question, 75.12 percent would like to receive additional training in using software for small-group instruction, and 50 teachers (24.88%) would not like to receive training in this strategy. At the 4-6 grade level, of the 146 teachers who responded, 73.97 percent would like training in this strategy and 26.03 would not. At the 7-8 grade level, 118 teachers responded, 60.17 percent of whom would like to receive training in using software for small group learning and 29.83 percent of whom would not like to receive training in this strategy. At the 9-12 grade level, of the 223 teachers who answered this question, 70.85 percent would like to receive training in using software for small-group cooperative learning activities and 29.15 percent would not. These differences yielded a chi-square value of 9.00, with $p = .03$.

Table 13. Teachers Wishing to Improve Their Computer Strategies in Using Software for Small Group Cooperative Learning.

Grade Level	Yes	No	Total
K-3			
N	151	50	201
%	75.12	24.88	100
4-6			
N	108	38	146
%	26.03	26.03	100
7-8			
N	71	47	118
%	60.17	39.83	100
9-12			
N	158	65	223
%	70.85	29.15	100

Note: χ^2 $(3, N = 688) = 9.00, p = .03$.

Survey Question 16: Using Software for Teacher-Directed Lessons

The results to Question 16 are reported in Table 14. Of the 201 grade K-3 teachers who responded to this queston, 61.19 percent would like to receive training in using software for teacher-directed lessons and 38.81 percent would not like to receive training in this strategy. Of the 146 teachers of grades 4-6 who responded to this question, 67.12 percent would like to receive training in this strategy and 32.88 percent would not. Of the 118 teachers of grades 7-8 who responded, 61.86 percent would like to receive training in using software for teacher-directed lessons and 38.14 would not like to receive training in this strategy. At the 9-12 grade level, 223 teachers responded to this question; 69.96 percent would like to receive training in this strategy and 30.04 percent would not. These differences yielded a chi-square value of 4.46, with $p = .22$.

Table 14. Teachers Wishing to Improve Their Computer Strategies in Using Software for Teacher-Directed Lessons.

Grade Level	Yes	No	Total
K-3			
N	123	78	201
%	61.69	38.31	100
4-6			
N	98	48	146
%	67.12	32.88	100
7-8			
N	73	45	18
%	61.86	38.14	100
9-12			
N	156	67	223
%	69.96	30.04	100

Note: χ^2 (3, $N = 688$) = 4.46, $p = .22$.

Survey Question 17: Developing Print Support Materials

The results to Question 17 are presented in Table 15. Of the 201 teachers grades K-3 who responded to this question, 56.22 percent would like to receive training in developing print support materials, while 88 (42.48%) indicated that they would not like to receive training in this strategy. At the grade 4-6 level, of the 146 teachers who responded to this question, 58.22 percent would like to receive training in this strategy and 41.78 percent would not. At the 7-8 grade level, of the 118 teachers who responded, 62.71 percent would like to receive training in this strategy and 37.92 percent would not like to receive training. At the grade level 9-12, of the 223 teachers who responded to this question, 70.85 percent would like to receive training in developing print support materials and 29.15 percent would not like to receive training in this strategy. These differences yielded a chi-square value of 11.16, with $p = .01$.

Table 15. Teachers Wishing to Improve Their Computer Strategies in Developing Print Support Materials.

Grade Level	Yes	No	Total
K-3			
N	113	88	201
%	56.22	43.78	100
4-6			
N	85	61	146
%	59.22	41.78	100
7-8			
N	44	44	118
%	37.29	37.29	100
9-12			
N	158	65	223
%	70.85	29.15	100

Note: χ^2 (3, $N = 688$) = 11.16, $p = .01$.

Survey Question 18: Teaching Students About Computers

The results to Question 18 are presented in Table 16. In grades K-3, 102 teachers responded to this question, of which 60.20 percent would like to receive training in teaching students about computers and 39.80 percent would not like to receive training in this strategy. At grade level 4-6, 146 teachers responded to this question; 54.79 percent would like to receive training in teaching students about computers and 45.21 percent would not. At grade level 7-8, of the 118 teachers who responded to this question, 39.83 percent would like to receive training in this strategy and 60.17 percent would not. At the 9-12 grade level, 223 teachers responded to this question, of which 34.08 would like to receive training in teaching students about computers and 65.92 percent would not. These differences yielded a chi-square value of 34.99, with $p = .00$.

Table 16. Teachers Wishing to Improve Their Computer Strategies in Teaching Students about Computers.

Grade Level	Yes	No	Total
K-3			
N	121	80	201
%	60.20	39.80	100
4-6			
N	80	66	146
%	54.79	45.21	100
7-8			
N	47	71	118
%	39.83	60.17	100
9-12			
N	76	147	223
%	34.08	65.92	100

Note: χ^2 $(3, N = 688) = 34.99, p = .00.$

Survey Question 19: Editing/Authoring Computer Software for Student Use

The results to Question 19 are presented in Table 17. Of the 201 teachers of grades K-3 who responded to this question, 34.83 percent would like to receive training in editing/authoring computer software for student use, and 65.17 percent would not like to receive training in this strategy. Of the 146 teachers of grade level 4-6 who responded to this question, 39.73 percent would like to receive training in this strategy and 60.27 would not like to receive training in editing/authoring computer software. At grade level 7-8, 201 teachers grade responded to this question, of whom 33.61 percent would like to receive training in this strategy and 66.39 percent would not. At grade level 9-12, 223 teachers responded to this question; 37.22 percent would like to receive training in editing/authoring computer software for student use and 62.78 percent would not like to receive training in this strategy. These differences yielded a chi-square value of 1.38, with $p = .71$.

Table 17. Teachers Wishing to Improve Their Computer Strategies in Editing/Authoring Computer Software for Student Use.

Grade Level	Yes	No	Total
K-3			
N	70	131	201
%	34.83	65.17	100
4-6			
N	58	88	146
%	39.73	60.27	100
7-8			
N	40	79	119
%	33.61	66.39	100
9-12			
N	83	140	223
%	37.22	62.78	100

Note: χ^2 (3, $N = 689$) = 1.38, $p = .71$.

Survey Question 20: Procedures for Evaluating Instructional Software

The results of Question 20 are presented in Table 18. Of the 201 teachers of grades K-3 who answered this question, 32.88 percent would like to receive training in procedures for evaluting instructional software and 67.16 would not like to receive training in this strategy. At the 4-6 grade level, 146 teachers responded to this question; 36.99 would like to receive training in this strategy and 63.01 percent would not like to receive training. At the 7-8 grade level, 118 teachers responded, 32.20 percent of whom would like to receive training in procedures for evaluating software for instructional use, and 56.95 percent would not. These differences yielded a chi-square value of 6.16, with $p = .10$.

Table 18. Teachers Wishing to Improve Their Computer Strategies in Procedures for Evaluating Instructional Software.

Grade Level	Yes	No	Total
K-3			
N	66	135	201
%	32.84	67.17	100
4-6			
N	54	92	146
%	36.99	63.01	100
7-8			
N	38	80	118
%	32.20	67.80	100
9-12			
N	96	127	223
%	43.05	59.95	100

Note: χ^2 (3, $N = 688$) = 6.16, $p = .10$.

Table 19. Summary of Teacher Responses Regarding Grade Levels at Which Improvement in Computer Strategies is Desired.

Question	Grade Level									
	K-3		4-6		7-8		9-12		Total	
	N	%	*N*	%	*N*	%	*N*	%	*N*	%
14. Using software, indiv. instr.	135	67	102	70	72	61	156	70	465	67.6
15. Using software, sm. groups	151	75	108	74	71	60	158	71	488	70.9
16. Software, teacher	123	61	98	67	73	62	156	70	450	65.4
17. Dev. print materials	113	56	85	58	74	63	158	71	430	62.5
18. Teaching students abt. computers	121	60	80	55	47	40	76	34	324	47.1
19. Editing/ authoring software, students	70	35	58	40	40	34	83	37	251	36.5
20. Evaluating instruct. software	66	33	54	37	38	32	96	43	254	36.6

Note: percentages are for "Yes" answers.

Question 7

At which grade level (K-3, 4-6, 7-8, or 9-12) do teachers spend the greatest percentage of time in direct classroom instruction with computers?

Survey Question 34 was used to answer this research question. The data are shown in Table 20. The percentages of the greatest computer use in direct classroom instruction are reported by grade level. The data are tabulated by hours and minutes on a weekly basis.

The chi-square value of 36.61, with $p = .00$, indicates a significant difference in the amount of time spent with students at different grade levels. The most time that teachers spend utilizing computers in direct classroom instruction is at the 9-12 grade level, with 15.56 percent of teachers spending one hour or more weekly with their students in direct classroom instruction utilizing computers. Only 1 percent of teachers at the K-3 level spend more than one hour per week utilizing computers in direct classroom instruction.

Table 20. Amount of Time Computers Are Used in Direct Classroom Instruction.

Grade Level	Time (minutes)				
	0	15-29	30-59	60+	Total
K-3					
N	159	32	8	2	201
%	79.10	15.92	3.98	1.00	100
4-6					
N	105	25	6	12	148
%	70.95	16.89	4.05	8.11	100
7-8					
N	93	13	1	9	116
%	80.17	11.21	0.86	7.76	100
9-12					
N	143	36	11	35	225
%	63.56	16.00	4.89	15.50	100

Note: χ^2 $(6, N = 690) = 36.61$, $p = .00$.

Question 8

At which level of computer skills (beginner, intermediate, advanced) do the greatest percent of teachers perceive themselves to be?

Survey Question 7 was used to answer this research question. The teachers' responses were tabulated for each of the categories (beginner, intermediate, and advanced) and percentages were computed. The data are organized from beginner to advanced by level of skills and are presented in Table 21. No statistical tests for significance were performed. The greatest percentage of teachers (61.80) are at the beginner level and the smallest percentage (8.0) are at the advanced level.

Table 21. Levels at Which Teachers Perceive Their Computer Skills ($N = 707$).

Skill	N
Beginner	437
Intermediate	233
Advanced	58

Question 9

In which ways do the greatest number of teachers utilize computers in their instruction?

Survey questions 35-39 were used to answer this research question. The numbers and percentages of teachers who utilize computers by area are listed in Table 22. No statistical tests for significance were performed. Computers are used by the greatest percentage of teachers (37.95) to supplement a lesson, followed by reinforcing lessons (36.95%); the smallest percentage (14.06%) of teachers use computers to introduce a lesson.

Table 22. Research Question 9, Survey Questions 35-39

Do you use computers in any of the following ways: to introduce a lesson, follow-up a lesson, to supplement lessons, to reinforce lessons, to teach about computers?

Question: Computer Use	Response			
	Yes		No	
	N	%	N	%
Q 35: Introduce lessons	97	14.06	593	86.94
Q 36 : Follow-up lessons	521	23.95	685	76.05
Q 37: Supplement	430	37.95	693	62.05
Q 38: Reinforce lessons	255	36.95	435	63.05
Q 39: Teach about computers	131	18.95	560	81.95

Note: $N = 728$.

Appendix C

BRIEF SUMMARY OF RESULTS

General Findings

The findings of this study indicate that the majority of teachers do not understand how to use computers in the teaching process, to utilize software, or to design instruction to integrate computers into the classroom instruction.

The majority of teachers do not understand how to utilize computers with students in actual classroom instructional situations, such as small group cooperative learning, individualized instruction, and teacher-directed learning situations, which are basic to the integration of computers into the instructional process.

The results of this study indicate a need to train teachers in actual student-centered instructional strategies and to design their instructional program of classroom teaching to integrate computers into the instructional process.

Specific Data

The majority of teachers believe that they are at the beginner level of computer use.

Less than one-tenth of the classroom teachers perceive themselves to be at the advanced level of computer skill.

Only 1 percent of teachers spend more than one hour per week utilizing computers in direct classroom instruction.

The greatest percentage of time that students spend on computers in the classroom was at the 4-6 and K-3 grade levels, and it is only 15-29 minutes per week. The lowest percentage of time that students spend using computers in their classroom instruction on a weekly basis was at the 7-8 grade and 9-12 levels, where at least half of the teachers report that students spend no time using computers in the classroom.

The greatest percentage of computer usage in direct classroom instruction was found among the resource teachers, with one-quarter responding that they use computers in direct classroom instruction for more than an hour on a weekly basis.

Mathematics was the subject that most utilized computers. 36.05 percent of teachers who use computers utilized them for mathematics instruction, while 32.09 percent of teachers who use computers to support instruction, utilized them for reading and writing.

Approximately two-thirds of teachers at the K-3 level would like to receive training to improve their personal computer skills. Teachers in the lower grades utilize computers a greater percentage of the time than do teachers in grades 9-12. Over half of 7-8 grade and 9-12 grade teachers also indicated an interest in improving their personal computer skills.

INDEX

ABOUT THE AUTHOR

Edith O'Donnell earned her Ed.D. in Instructional Technology and her M.L.S. in Library and Information Science at the University of Southern California, and her M.A. in Instructional Technology at California State University, Long Beach. She holds credentials in the following areas: Secondary Administration and Supervisory, Community College Instructor, Community College Librarian and Supervisory, and Secondary Teaching and School Library Media. She has worked in the field of education since 1959. She has taught at the university and community college levels, served as Library Media Director in California public schools, and was a consulting writer for the State of California Department of Education, Library and Learning Resources Department. She has conducted seminars at state, local, and national computer and school media conferences, received a grant to produce and host educational television talk shows for cable television, and was a delegate to the Governor of California's Conference in preparation for the President's White House Conference on Libraries and Information Science. Edith has served on the California School Library Association Southern Executive Board in several capacities, and on numerous library media committees. She is currently an educational research consultant, author, and educational talk show producer and host. Previous publications include *Library Media Classes at Los Altos High School: The First Stride Toward Future Excellence; Programmed Instruction for the Reader's Guide to Periodical Literature; Library Media Technical Assistant Analysis Handbook* (with California State Community College Task Analysis Committee); *The Data Bank: A Service of the Legal Services Committee, California School Library Association;* and *Handbook for Teaching Library Media Skills in Secondary Schools.*